MW01613441

I LIFT MY LAMP

BY ALBERTA SMITH

IN COLLABORATION WITH
MAUDE ALLISON LATHEM

Published by
METAPHYSICAL SCIENCE ASSOCIATION
P. O. Box 6514, Metropolitan Station
Los Angeles, California

LOS ANGELES
INSTITUTE OF RELIGIOUS SCIENCE
1938

Copyright 1937, by
ALBERTA SMITH,
Los Angeles, California

Second Edition

Printed in the United States of America
By KELLAWAY-IDE COMPANY
Los Angeles, California

To

My husband,

FRANK BAKER SMITH

"Thy word is a lamp unto my feet, and a light unto my path."

Psalms 119:115

CONTENTS

FOREWORD

THE complaint has been registered, in many sections of the country, that too little of personal experience in spiritual growth is ever given to the public, by those who are in position to impart this knowledge. In every other line of activity, it appears that all persons who have achieved greatly try to leave intimate accounts of the workings of their minds through the course of their struggle. But great spiritual leaders leave scant information as to their fears and conflicts, and yet, it is thought, these struggles must be similar to ours, and therefore a knowledge of them would be helpful.

Thousands of books are printed, dealing with all the complex problems, political, social, economic, and moral, that immediately confront the world today. In this book, the author makes no attempt to solve all of these, but she cannot escape the feeling that over and above all else, people need more of the knowledge of the spirit which transforms men's lives. The only possible reason the author, in this instance, could have for the presentation of the book you are about to read, is the hope that, from her experience in proving God, some reader may be convinced that there is a Power in the universe which responds to our need — which turns to us as we turn to It.

Religious leaders, alone, have not been responsible for the public remaining in ignorance as to the technique by which results are obtained in growth of spiritual life. Too often the world has shown its unwillingness to read or listen to a message delivered right from the heart. In order to insure an attentive ear, the message must be classified as either "psychology" or "romance." So, we have tried to formulate our ideas into easily credible forms, and in so doing we have attenuated them, so that little of anything is left to believe. Truth adulterated in this manner was sometimes clothed in vesture so opaque that the world hardly responded above a slow pulsation.

I am anxious that we shall not be confused by terminology. Whether I speak of God as Creator, Truth or Mind, I am referring to the vital Principle of life. Since It is All-Presence, we can contact it wherever we are. The Bible tells us that the word is not afar off but in our own mouth. What we need now is to learn how to use this word, so that we shall become creative centers within ourselves.

We care less and less about defining God, but

we are tremendously concerned with experiencing for ourselves the immediate consciousness of God within the soul. We study the Law of Attraction, somewhere in this book, and by this law, we know that the thing to which we give attention becomes a part of our consciousness. And the man who earnestly desires to know God *will succeed*, and he will find the real God right within himself.

What the world needs today is not to have more of Truth stated but to be willing to abide by that which is already known. As a matter of fact, practically all of the Christian Churches are agreed, so far as their *statements* regarding God are concerned, but it would seem that there is not always responsibility felt in the matter of the individual application of these truths. The common misapprehension seems to be that God is omnipotent in a potential manner, but not in any actual sense. In other words, that He has the power if He chooses to use it; that evil exists because God permits it, and so mankind is afflicted by divine consent. A God not wholly good would never satisfy me. Would it you?

Our teaching is that God is "the same yesterday, today and forever," and that His nature is *always* Good, and that He is as incapable of diminishing His omnipotence, that evil might become real, as He is of committing evil!

There is no attempt to make this book either scholarly or ecclesiastical. While it is my hope that it may contain some food satisfying to the deeply metaphysical mind, at the same time, it is my desire and purpose to state things so simply, that anyone reading for the first time about the ever-availability of God, will feel an urge to seek Him. I have naturally embodied here such principles as I have taught all of my students, both in classes and in private work. Primarily, I believe I am writing this for my students. As I begin writing, I immediately think of the problems they have brought me for solution, and in attempting to solve these, perhaps I shall answer other questions as well.

We have been accused, in our system of thought, of being so persistently optimistic that we have no comprehension of the troubles which come to humanity — that we even ignore them. This accusation completely misses the mark. We are grateful, however, that we have created the impression of an optimistic attitude. We admit this.

But this optimism comes wholly from the fact that we have proven that there is no condition in which we find ourselves which cannot be changed by our attitude toward it. Alchemists have, for centuries, believed that they would one day learn how to change the baser metals into gold. Whether they have yet been able to do this, is not our concern at the moment, but we are thoroughly convinced that it is possible for human beings to change conditions in themselves, and in their surroundings, to something entirely different. Not only is it possible, but it is being done daily.

If we can intelligently comprehend the fact that *real man* is never sick and cannot be sick, we shall be able to impress subjective mind with this truth (since subjective mind, as we shall learn later on, knows only to execute the orders given it by our conscious mind) and the experience of a perfect body will be manifested in our lives. Maybe I should pause right here to explain that we, of course, teach there is but One Mind, and this the Mind of Christ, and that this is the mind you use and the mind I use, but to more specifically convey our thought, we refer to that which we *consciously* think as being the action of our conscious mind and that thinking which goes on unconsciously as being done by our subjective mind. In reality, there is only one Mind.

When we come to understand that evil is but a negation, like darkness, having no real substance or place; that God is all there is, this knowledge will enable us to see, once and for all, that evil is a delusion, without power or presence, and it is as silly to spend our time in fighting it, as it would be to waste our strength in combatting a shadow. Then we shall be able to adopt the Christ method of non-resistance to evil, and "turn upon it the light of pure goodness and keep it there persistently until the darkness is converted into light."

The author is greatly indebted to Ernest Holmes for permission to quote from his textbook, *Science of Mind.* Also, to Josephine Holmes Curtis, Editor, *Science of Mind Magazine,* to which publication I make frequent reference. I have, of course, used freely that which, from its very nature, may be regarded as more or less common property. For instance, I might write in here "God is love." That expression would not be mine alone, for it has been used by hundreds of people. So, many of the principles of metaphysics are alike the common property of lecturers, students, writers, and teachers. When these truths have been used by me, I have attempted to invest them with an original vigor and then have used them as if I alone of all the world had ever thought of them. They will only call forth a response from you, if you have felt, somewhere in the hazy background of your consciousness, a longing for something of their nature. If I am able to transform for you that transitory inspiration into a real conviction; if I can assist you, mentally and spiritually, in passing from the realm of nebulous suggestion to that of valid experience, then, indeed, this book will have served its purpose. Then, indeed, we shall be able to sing with the psalmist David: "For thou wilt light my candle; the Lord my God will enlighten my darkness."

ALBERTA SMITH.

February 27, 1937.

INTRODUCTION

WHETHER or not thought is creative is no longer a subject remaining in the field of debate: it is an accepted fact. With this far-reaching fact confronting us — that thought is creative — it behooves us to fortify ourselves by learning the technique of its operation. In a recent sermon, a local divine said: "Healing is a legitimate and urgent function of the church. Physical and mental health is an integral, vital part of the Christian program for every life. Faith, love and peace are healing agents."*

With the general tendency of modern times, both in and out of the church, it is certainly not amiss to have a metaphysical teacher, of the demonstrated ability of Alberta Smith, put into book form the technique by which she works. Mrs. Smith is a clear and concise teacher, a sincere and enthusiastic exponent of Religious Science.

Truth's appearing is seldom in accord with preconceived opinions, but man's progress is always in proportion to his obedience to his light,

*Dr. Sheldon Shepard.

17

the lamp within his soul, the law of God. Owing to environment, education and inclination, there are honest differences of opinion as to what is truth; and we believe and teach that everyone should have perfect freedom to make the discovery for himself. The liberated teacher never attacks another's beliefs, never seeks to proselyte, nor tries to force his opinions upon others — but he does have a reason for the faith which is within him, which he is ready to impart to each and all who come to him.

The lessons in this book are based upon a belief in a divine, self-existent Life — and man's oneness with it — as primal as life, as lasting as eternity. We believe that Mind is more than an attribute of Deity, that Mind is God; and it is through this understanding of the oneness and allness of Mind, and man's unity with It, that we seek to heal the sick, to comfort the sorrowful, and to enlarge the experience of our objective limitations.

For ten years or more, Mrs. Smith has maintained an office at our Institute, has taught in our classes and contributed to our magazine, and hundreds have been blessed through her ministrations. She *knows* in Whom she has believed, and her confident assurance has brought peace to many troubled minds. Through her years of loving, patient work, Mrs. Smith has endeared herself to all of us, and we feel has brought nearer the spiritual vision of John on Patmos: "There shall be no more curse . . . and there shall be no more light there; and they need no candle, neither light of the sun; for the Lord God giveth them light and they shall reign for ever and ever."

I know that this book will go forth as a beacon light to many minds and may God bless both it and its author.

ERNEST HOLMES, *Dean,*
Institute of Religious Science.

February, 1937

CHAPTER 1

Who Does Your Thinking?

THIS question would be easy to answer if one lived in Italy, Germany, or Greece. One might not be expected to do his own thinking: it is being done for him! But, what about those of us in this "land of the free and home of the brave," who does our thinking? You say that answer is easy. "Of course, *I do my own thinking*," you reply. But, do you?

It is becoming increasingly plain to all reflecting minds that most of us try to escape any responsibility which requires us to think. We act as if we were afraid of the mind which has been given us and spend half of our time trying to avoid the use of it. Perhaps one in fifty has the initiative, and the courage, to think things through to a logical conclusion, while we of the remaining forty-nine follow each other like sheep, going to almost any lengths to keep from thinking for ourselves. That is why so many of us are poor, incompetent and without enthusiasm, and why

21

many of us will progress no further than our predecessors.

Yet, it is surely a fact, the present generation accepts, almost without question, the statement that "He can who *thinks* he can."

Most of us would develop more efficient thinking processes, if we were aware of how much our thought is influenced both by emotion and habit. We acquire, in some manner, certain fixed beliefs about a subject, and when new facts bearing on this subject are brought to our attention, our impulse is to classify these according to our fixed opinion, rather than to interpret them on a basis of truth. This is being biased by the *habit* of our thought. This is a splendid way to obstruct original thinking.

I believe most of us, even if we concede that thought is creative, labor under the delusion that our thoughts are creative *only* when we decide they shall be. We go along through the day, attending to our routine duties, and then suddenly we say to ourselves, "I had better stop and give my husband a treatment," and for about thirty minutes we endeavor to see the perfection of man, the goodness of God and man's unity with it; but for the other twelve or fourteen hours of our working moments, we have allowed our minds to be filled with every sort of denial of good . . . lack of money, lack of time, lack of friends, lack of opportunity. What would you say was doing our thinking, the right attitude of mind, in which we lived for thirty minutes, or the seven or eight hundred minutes in which our consciousness was filled with negative thoughts? I don't need answer that for you.

It is exactly as if we made a wax phonograph record, perhaps recording a beautiful poem. A few minutes later, we play into it a few bars of jazz, and from that we go to a reading of Hamlet's soliloquy, and at the end of the day we put our record on the victrola because we want to hear the beautiful poem again. Where has it gone? All that remains is a confused babble. Certain it is that subjective mind is executing the *dominant* impression given it. So, if sick thoughts dominate our consciousness the major portion of our time, then sickness is doing our thinking for us!

A belief in sickness and lack has been the thief which has stolen from us our priceless heritage, and it remains for us to change our thinking and increase our consciousness of the God within. It will do us small good to reiterate the statement that God is omnipresent, omniscient, and omnipotent, if our belief — the deepest thoughts of our being — is that we still have to fight sickness and lack. Poverty and sickness are doing our thinking for us as long as this is true.

If you are not getting the results out of life which you believe you should, which you are certain you desire from life, then, no matter how much you claim to recognize the Allness of Good, YOU ARE NOT DOING YOUR OWN THINK-ING! We know this is true, for the promises still hold: "As a man thinketh in his heart, so is he," . . . "Ask and ye shall receive," and so on. If you are not reaping *what you are under the impression you are sowing,* look into your thinking. Perhaps worry is doing your thinking for you. For centuries, worry has been saying to man that God is *not* a "present help in time of trouble." He had a basic belief that God *was* ever-present, but he did not have a complete embodiment of that which he desired — the mental equivalent. He did not maintain, with all the force of his being that Good was continuously operative in his life, and Worry stepped in and did his thinking for him! If worry is doing our thinking for us, it is doing it by robbing us of a sense of God. Worry has been called a *wavering* belief. James says that "he that wavereth is like a wave of the sea, driven with the wind and tossed." Let's not let worry rob us of our good, do our thinking for us.

When you answer me that you do your own thinking, I am certain you believe you do, but most of us do not think for ourselves. If you answer me that it is your *right* to do your own thinking, then 1 shall agree with you whole-heartedly. It is our right, perhaps the greatest of all God-given privileges — the right of free choice. We can use this power to bring about our destruction or we can use it to produce healing, prosperity, joy, happiness — all the results of renewing our minds, thinking in a God-like manner. Paul says we are to be transformed by the renewing of our minds.

But, something in human nature makes us reluctant to change our minds. Nor do we want another to change our mind for us, nor will we even face the fact that the unpleasant condition in which we find ourselves is, in any way, the result of our thinking. My friends, there is no other way out. Ages ago, the Hebrew poet sang

"Thou wilt keep him in perfect peace whose mind is stayed on thee." This is the only certain way of salvation we have ever learned. If consciousness is impregnated with the unshaken belief that God is within, worry cannot disturb our thinking; a belief of lack will not make an impression upon us, and health will be such a reality that sickness will be outside our ken. Let us not, however, in our earnestness to reach out after God, make the mistake of going *beyond* Him, as it were, by confusing the "within" as a starting point, rather than the continuous dwelling place of God.

All of these points are by the way of stimulating your interest in the one subject of this book — Creative Mind. "An attempt to explain what each soul must discover for himself: that he stands in the midst of an eternal creative Power, which presses Itself around his own thought, and casts back to him, glorified, all that he thinks." Every word in this book is an attempt to show you that there is no item of life exempt from individual domination. If it is prosperity you are seeking, then our talk with you will be on creative Mind and prosperity; if it is happiness you want above all else, then our remarks will deal with creative

26

Mind and happiness, for Mind is God, and *is the One Causation back of everything.*

If there is but One Mind, then we must agree that our thought is the activity of that One Mind in our consciousness, and this Power is not only as great as the power that holds the planets in their place, *it is the very same Power.* So, no matter how disagreeable the task, we must admit the truth to ourselves: whatever the condition in which we find ourselves at this moment, it was created by the activity of thought, and sustained by a belief in its reality. Thus, the condition grew out of a conviction or opinion — which was a thing of thought — so, we can deprive this condition of its life blood, can deprive it of any semblance of reality, by simply withdrawing our belief in it. We are not bound by any preconceived opinion, which may have given birth to undesirable conditions; and we need not regard ourselves as bound to any intolerable state of affairs. All old things are immediately made new if we have a mind that welcomes growth.

The worst misfortune that could befall us would be for us not to recognize the creative power of Mind. Having recognized it, the next greatest misfortune would be to set the time of Its operation at some future date. This does nothing but impress upon Infinite Wisdom — which knows only the eternal Now — our conviction that a betterment of conditions for us is deferred. (Creative Mind has nothing to do but to give back to us what we have thought.) If we say to ourselves: "Things are pretty terrible now, but they are going to be better next month," we are merely saying that today Evil is a power but next month God will come home and take over the reins of the government. Have you ever stopped to ask yourself the question "What is it that will make God powerful next month, which He is lacking today?" The only authentic information we have on this subject is that "God is the same, yesterday, today and forever." If you get only one thought from this book and that thought be: *there is no stability in life until we put from us the thought that God can change*, it will be worth all my effort to have given you this re-vivifying consciousness.

If it be true, and it must be, that man is a center of intelligence in the great Universal Mind, and that every time he thinks, he sets mind into action, shall it not profit us this day, and every day, to allow our thoughts to dwell on those things which are of good report, which are in line with divine Wisdom? Most of us try to make ourselves as presentable as possible physically; most of us refuse to make friends of thieves and outlaws; most of us refrain from entertaining in our homes either adults or children who will wreck our furniture, pour ink on our carpets, mutilate our paintings and break our china.

But what about the thoughts we harbor? Shall we not realize that it is worthwhile to "stand porter at the door of thought," that no thief may enter and steal from us our peace of mind? Shall we not find it more profitable to think only on those things which are "of good report," so that we need have no anxieties about the results? Shall we not, right this moment, turn our desires into convictions, and give to infinite creative Mind a positive acceptance of all the good which we wish now to experience? Shall we not calmly but certainly know, that which is inspired thought sets in motion an all-creative, receptive medium, which carries out our instructions? If our word is thus sustained and manifested by a universal ever-present law, and we are what we believe ourselves to be, by reason of the fact that Mind honors our self-estimate, then can we not see clearly that we are independent creators of our bodies and our affairs? This becomes an obvious fact, if the potency of our conviction is not weakened by finite preoccupation with fear and failure.

Doesn't this bring home to us why we need constantly to remember Solomon's injunction: "With all thy getting, get understanding." Since subjective mind is the one location our instructions are not questioned, where we do not have to gain anyone's consent to the law we are about to make for ourselves, we must know whether we are acting wisely or foolishly; we must be certain that we want to live with the things which we are creating by our thought. How imperative it becomes that we keep our thinking on that strata which is affirmative, constructive, and in line with reality!

Peace, health, abundance, happiness and all affirmative qualities exist by virtue of their eternal reality. Just where we are, right now, no matter how great the external confusion, there is that place within where all is still. To enter this peaceful center is communion with God, and into this sanctuary, we cannot carry a thought of fear, worry, lack, or of any confusion. As the roots of our being are fed from this life center, we become impervious to strife. This must have been what Shakespeare meant when he said: "Rest is not quitting the busy career. 'Tis the brook's onward motion, clear, without strife." Strife comes about from resistance, from combatting people and conditions which we think are unfavorable to us. Peace is an attribute of God. The One, Eternal, and Infinite Essence of life must be at peace, for there is no power opposed to It, with which It could be at war. We have, then, only to turn our thoughts to the recognition of that peace of God, which is within us, and we are able to see not only our own Divinity, but that of every other man, and are able to recognize God in every form and expression of life.

Since we can now understand why we can experience any good for ourselves which we are able to *think*, we grasp the meaning of the Bible promise "Lift up now thine eyes . . . for all the land which thou seest to thee will I give it . . . " and "Every place whereon the soles of your feet shall tread, shall be yours." All that we can mentally *see*, we can manifest in our lives. Since we are one with Good, fulfillment is assured to us of necessity. If Spirit, which cannot be limited to, nor described by, finite understanding is perfect; then, since It is my sustainer, I, too, must forever be perfect, forever be perfectly supplied . . . "All the land which thou seest."

In view of all this, shall we let anything other than Infinite Wisdom do our thinking? Right thinking is all powerful because it is aligned with Truth. Thoughts of Power and Strength build up a consciousness of might, mastery and dominion, and overcome every negative appearance. In the realm of Reality, where "The Lord God Omnipotent reigneth," there can be no poverty of thought, and he who is awake to the divine possibilities, may prove, beyond a shadow of doubt, that God is always pouring out His richest blessings.

If one's motives, in seeking and giving, are pure, his blessings will increase in proportion to his understanding and faith. So, it is our task to climb the heights of holiness. Let us then start on our upward journey, full of faith and expectation, unified as a whole with the Indwelling Christ — the great and mighty I AM within. Man is a center of individualized divine consciousness, thinking into mind each day that which he wishes manifested in his daily experiences. "We are dealing with Creative Mind, and when man realizes that everything is Mind; and that nothing moves but Mind, and that the only instrument is thought, he will see that nothing can permanently heal but right thinking." Thus shall we keep sacred the integrity of our own soul, thus shall we shut out any doubts or fears which would mar the realization of our Divine status.

CHAPTER II

The Magnifying Glass of Praise

IT IS NOT by accident that the word PRAISE occurs so many times in the Bible. Nor does it always convey the same meaning. In the greater number of instances, the thought of worship — the act of glorifying God — is indicated. Next in importance seems to be the idea of commendation for worth or excellence; and, then, a close alliance with the word *gratitude*, carrying the thought of a warm, friendly feeling toward a benefactor; and, in many instances, the thought of *magnifying* is distinctly implied.

Have you ever stopped to think how little progress could have been made in the scientific world, if there had been no instruments with which to magnify the objects under observation? But for the powerful telescope, we should likely have remained in ignorance of the planets for many more years. Without a magnifying lense, biological research could never have accomplished the beneficent results with which it has been credited. So, there is no denying the fact that the magnifying glass occupies a position of importance in the world.

It is no less important to man when he is working entirely in the realm of thought. (He soon finds that to attain spiritual growth, it is necessary to magnify the good which he now has, in order to insure a rapid increase. The magnifying glass he uses is PRAISE. New students of Truth, so happy, so full of joy, so eager to give thanks for every blessing, think they have made an original discovery when they learn that their good is increasing through the activity of praise. They report that praise has the power to bring out of the seeming void, the very thing for which they pray. And they are certain the fact has just been revealed!

Yet the wonder-working power of prayer and praise was well illustrated when the shackles fell from Paul and Silas, as they were confined "in the inner prison and their feet in stocks." Paul had the perfect faith. He said: "For I am persuaded that neither death nor life, nor angels nor principalities, nor powers, nor things present, nor things to come; nor height nor depth, nor any other creature, shall be able to separate us from the love of God, which is in Christ Jesus our Lord." (Rom. 8:38, 39). An understanding such as this was tremendous then, and such faith in the perfect operation of God's law is tremendous now. This was the real *magnifying glass of praise* — the faith that accepted his deliverance as a present fact, while he was yet in chains!

What has been the effect of such praise as you have heard, merely praise for the kindly gestures of life? Has it made people better or worse? Most of us feel that the action of praise is magical. Even praising the good deeds of a child causes him to want to be good . . . to want to be worthy of your praise. He thrives under praise. His consciousness is exalted through it. This would seem to be in line with Bulwer's comment on the subject: "How a little praise warms out of a man the good that is in him, as the sneer of contempt (which he feels is unjust) chills the ardor to excel."

A generation ago parents did not have so much information on the subject of praise. A man of splendid attainments told me recently that the inhibiting tendencies of his youth had handicapped him in all the experiences of life because in his youth he was never permitted to think anything he did was above the average. Praise of himself was unthinkable. He carries now a vivid impression of being shocked when he was about eight years old by hearing the cook relate how entertaining she had been the night before until everyone had pronounced her "the life of the party." It was so foreign to his innate sense of refinement, that fifty years later he still carries a distinct impression of the shock.

A woman of eighty-five, who had reared a family of ten, told me it was with much regret that she recognized now, when they were all grown, that she had stood in the way of their fuller development by denying them praise. To one of her devout mind, praise meant a flattery of the personality, a catering to vanity; and, praying that they might be Godlike, her effort was to prevent them from "thinking too highly of themselves." In this day of great personal achievement, when most people are assured they can accomplish whatever they wish; and in the distance we have gone from the old theological concepts, we can hardly visualize a time when the training was to keep children from being too smart. Evidently, that dear woman was not familiar with Bovee's sentiments that: "Words of praise, indeed, are almost as necessary to warm a child into a congenial life as are acts of kindness and affection. Judicious praise is to children what sun is to the flowers."

What a contrast, when we think of how we are urged to bring forth the divinity within us! We are even taught to say "wonderful, wonderful, wonderful me," being an expression of gratitude for the knowledge that we are God, expressing Himself as us, at the point of our intelligence. Shouldn't this evoke songs of praise?

John Ruskin, so anxious that every word he wrote might prove a blessing, said:

"You will find that it is less easy to uproot faults than to choke them by gaining virtues. Do not think of your faults, still less others' faults. In every person who comes near you, look for what is good and strong. Honor that, rejoice in it, and, as you can, try to imitate; and your faults will drop off, like dead leaves when their time comes."

So, it would appear that even these superficial results of praise would thoroughly justify its practice, even with people who know nothing of the laws of Mind. But with Religious Scientists, who are attempting to demonstrate their oneness with divine Mind, the necessity for praise in their daily lives is imperative. Right here, we are reminded that Steele says: "Whatever you *commend*, add your reasons for doing so; it is this which distinguishes the approbation of a man of sense from the flattery of sycophants and the admiration of fools." Since we would not come under the latter qualification, we hope to make it plain *why* we praise both ourselves and others.

The first great vista that opens up to us as students of Truth is the conviction that there is but One Mind, One Spirit, One Substance —only One Ultimate Reality, but within this One are many experiences. If God is all there is, and God cannot think or know anything unlike Himself, then, the *laws of God* govern our thinking. As God sees us perfect, we must forever see the Real Man as perfect, whether we are thinking of ourselves or another. This is the reason for our premise. An attitude of praise is putting the law of God's love into action, and love is manifest as life. There is an immutable law that if we, either by criticizing or by withholding praise, withdraw from our fellow men, we cut the cords of love which bind us . . . "sever the arteries and veins through which universal life flows."

40

To those who have not thought deeply on the subject, it may appear inconsistent, this praising a quality which is not apparent, but it is divinely consistent in reality. Praise of another's good qualities which do not seem to be evident, is compelling in ourselves an affirmation of the Truth of Being, and is forcing us to see only the perfect man. The mere fact of giving this expression destroys any seeds of envy and jealousy. The more difficult it is for us to form true concepts of others, the more determined we should be. For we have already learned, by this time, another great law: *That which we recognize as being a reality in any man's experience, may become a reality in our own!*

In Infinite Mind, every individual is motivated by an ultimate picture of perfection, though we are all at different stages of unfoldment. If we are searchers for the divinity in another, it is easy to find something to praise, and certainly this is true homage — praising God in humanity. We are not speaking now of the fulsome praise of the flatterer, but rather of that praise which comes *from* the Soul and is *of* and *to* the Soul. This praise forever heals, strengthens and inspires.

41

It is obvious that criticism is the exact antithesis of praise, as criticism insists on magnifying the discord. In criticising, we are wrong in two ways. First, we are setting ourselves up as judges, giving the impression by our fault-finding that we are without fault. Secondly, we are expressing personal standards of what is right, expecting others to follow. Our critical attitude at once proclaims *our* standard as an unsafe one to follow. The standard of Christ can be our only standard by which to judge both ourselves and others. But, *when we perceive this standard, we are wholly unable to criticize!* We can see only perfection, as God sees perfection. Criticism always displays the fact that we lack the power to behold the perfection of God!

The Mantle of Love is that garment of Praise described by the prophet Isaiah (61:3) as the gift of Christ. It is thrown over all the canvas of evil, proving how it is possible to sing praises for the good rather than to complain about the evil. The Christ in us should enable us to throw the garment of praise over the disconsolate, and often, by one little word, fan into flame the dying fires of self-respect and aspiration. As one only needs to keep the mouth and nose out of water, at times, to keep from drowning, so many times a slight lifting of the thought, a word of inspiration, a look or a handclasp — all expressions of praise — may restore the entire being to a state of true consciousness and equilibrium.

Praise is the outer edge — the fringe — of love, and love is the most potent factor in life. We must go right on magnifying the good in our mind, our body, and in our affairs. If we sow the seed, we shall reap a rich reward in health and prosperity and all good. We must not spare the words of praise, even when appearances indicate the opposite result, but must expect that our word will return filled with the truth of Spirit. As Carlyle said: "If there is a harvest ahead, it is poor thrift to be stingy with your seed corn."

Having proved beyond cavil the presence of the healing Christ, why should Religious Scientists be criticized for expecting this Mind to operate in their lives; and for giving thanks and *praising* that good which is not yet manifest? Man is inclined to praise God only when conditions and circumstances are so pleasant that praise is natural and spontaneous. We should bear in mind that Jesus always gave thanks *in advance*, before he even made his request, as in the raising of Lazarus and also in feeding the five thousand. His system was: "Enter into his gates with thanksgiving, and into his court with praise."

Without fear of contradiction, we claim that praise has the power to cause our good to increase and multiply! By praising that good which we now have — whether it be money, health, friends, or wisdom — we know we are causing that good to flourish. This is in accordance with law: the operation of the Law of Attraction. In "Creative Mind and Success," Ernest Holmes says: "We will always attract to ourselves, in our lives and conditions, according to our thought. See only that which you wish to experience. You can attract only that which you first mentally become and feel yourself to be in reality . . . The reason we can make our requests known *with thanksgiving, is because we know from the beginning that we are to receive,* and therefore we cannot help being thankful . . . So, let us cultivate all the gratitude we can. In gratitude, we will send our thought out into the world, and as it comes back it will come laden with the fruits of the Spirit."

As teachers and practitioners, we are compelled to use this magnifying glass of praise in making our demonstrations. If we think of happiness and health as belonging to the future, then we have entered the consciousness in which limitations have a part. The eternal now belongs to the consciousness which is untouched by limitation, in which fulfillment has already taken place — the time of the Spirit, the time of demonstration. If we are unable to praise God for the blessing which we know is ours, until it becomes visible on the objective plane, then our demonstration will always take place in the future. As B. F. Whitney says: "Your demonstrations will be put off until tomorrow, *it if takes you until tomorrow to get into the consciousness of the now.*"

As we are filled with the consciousness of "Now are we the sons of God . . . " we understand the *why* of constant praise. Can you imagine the Son of God giving to persons or things or conditions the power to deprive him of happiness? If the knowledge of your divine sonship does not bring forth songs of praise and thanksgiving, what would make you happy? As the son of God, you are not inferior to any other person in the world, nor is any other person inferior to you. Personal limitation has ceased to exist. With

45

this knowledge, can you do otherwise than forever praise the divinity which you recognize in
your fellow man? Resting in this spiritual realization, you are saying to every man you meet "The
Christ in me greets the Christ in you — the perfect man," and this magic formula of praise will
bless every man, woman and child who comes
within the periphery of your thoughts.

This ability to understand and obey Truth is
ours today, if we are ready to recognize and use it.
We sometimes forget that we neither make nor
sustain the truth. Actually, the most we can do
is to come into agreement with it; start the operation of it in our lives. Christ Jesus said: "Ye
shall know the truth and the truth shall make
you free." It is ours to affirm the truth and leave
God to operate it. We are all cultivators of our
own garden of thought, and it remains with us
"to will and to do." It is up to us to decide
whether it shall be a garden of weeds or a garden
of flowers. The difference is not so much one of
personal capacity as of consecration and devotion. God's demand is that man shall know only
good, and the difficulty of mortals in meeting it
is measured by the tenacity with which they hold
to a sense of evil.

A young, aeronautical engineer found himself very unhappy in his position with one of the large airplane manufacturing companies. Notwithstanding the fact that he had majored in engineering, and his chief interest in college had been airplanes, the work now seemed monotonous, tiresome and comparatively unremunerative, and the boy grew to hate it so strongly that he asked a practitioner to aid him in securing entirely different work.

He was told if he really wanted to get out of his present work, he would have to begin by praising it. That appeared thoroughly inconsistent to the boy, whose paramount thought was to escape from the present position and find a more congenial one. But the boy was intelligent and when it was shown how the law of attraction works, not only by increasing any recognized qualities, but by tying to us even more securely that which our mind dwells upon (even if this thought is one of hate) he saw quickly that it was imperative that he change his attitude and praise his present work.

So, he set about daily to discover everything good he could about it. It became a game with him and he was *so* surprised at the many things he found to praise. He had been shown that, in the realm of spirit(all the qualities or conditions which we desire are now present and belong as much to us as when we shall see them objectified.) He began to express, mentally, his praise for all the qualities which he desired in a superior officer. He wrote down a list of everything he could possibly appreciate, whether manifest or unmanifest, and daily praised these things.

The results were almost breath-taking. In about ten days, he came back with the report that his work had become so delightful, he wondered if he *should* change to another field of endeavor and waste all the time he had spent in preparation for this work. The practitioner explained to him that no time was ever wasted; that his only task now was(to continue with joyful heart; that if he put sufficient gratitude and praise into his work, *he would either bring out in his present position everything good he wanted, or he would be lifted out of that position into the one which did hold his desires!)* But the only lever he could use was love and praise.

In three weeks time, he received an offer from a larger concern, but the same kind of work, with an *increase* in salary of *fifty per cent of his entire present salary.* He accepted the offer, was placed in a different branch of the work, and later reported: "I have never found work so interesting. No play was ever so fascinating. Every day is a grand adventure and the hours simply fly by. At last I am in my right place, with unlimited opportunity ahead. God bless you for teaching me <u>how to spiritually lift</u> myself out of a monotonous work by <u>gratitude and praise!</u>"

Such testimonies are the proofs that we dare not relinquish so valuable an aid as praise.

There is, strangely enough, in human nature an inherent disposition to descant upon the subject of discord (whether it be the flood or the 'flu) and a disinclination to believe in the reality of good. There seems to be a stubborn determination to call evil good and to magnify it far above the good — an inclination to think negatively, to look for discord, to prophesy and expect it, and even to make mental laws that it shall come to pass, in hundreds of ways.

With the inconsistent belief that God knows both evil and good; that He is responsible for evil as well as good; and that it is His will for man to suffer — with such a delusive panorama constantly in view, what could be expected other

49

than a magnified sense of evil in all its myriad forms. As followers of Christ, it devolves upon us to magnify the good. It is essential that we accept as real only such thoughts as are traceable to divine Mind. There being only One Mind, there is, in reality, only one quality of thought, and this should be our constant declaration. Every right thought has an immaculate origin and expresses eternal life.

We are expressing perfect Principle when we praise God for blessings that are real on the spiritual plane this moment. The basic rule for spiritual growth which Jesus gave us was . . . "if any man will do his will, he shall know of the doctrine whether it be of God . . . " The "open sesame" to a practical proof of divine power — "If any man do his will." Can we fail to magnify with praise as we think of that? Is it wealth we are looking for? Real substance is certainly spir-itual. Is it happiness we think we desire? That is obviously a quality of the soul. Is it peace, poise, harmony, joy, wisdom or strength we are searching? These are certainly found in Mind.

Do you ever ask yourself, "why do I pray?" I will tell you. First, we pray because we have come to the end of our rope, as it were — recognized our own inadequacy. Secondly, we *believe* that God can help. Why should we think that God could or would answer prayer; on what is our belief founded? Is it not because of all the promises contained in the Scriptures, and because of the examples which Jesus gave us as to the manner of our praying? I think this is true. If we agree, then you will not dispute the statement that we cannot lay hold of part of the promises and disregard the others. One of the most important announcements of all time is: *"Before they call,* I will answer." According to this, before we have been able to express in words the desire of our heart, God has already answered! If this be true, then almost our first step in prayer must be to PRAISE Him! And again: "All things whatsoever ye shall ask in prayer, believing, ye shall receive." I think none of us would intentionally doubt God, yet *when we do not believe that He has answered even before we can ask, we are doubting God!*

A realization of the actual presence of God, of the fact that we "live and move and have our being in Him," enables us to eliminate from consciousness any belief that man can ever be less than perfect. Praise and gratitude are potent antidotes to any false belief of lack or discord. Gratitude just naturally flows into our consciousness as we become aware of the infinitude of good which that Presence insures. Thus, it is clearly manifest, as every man is seen by us as God sees him — kind, loving, tender, gracious, beautiful— we will, by this recognition, by this praise, be bringing harmony into our individual world.

Superstition, sensuality, and ignorance are still engaged in a determined effort to hold man in bondage to the belief in two powers — one good and the other evil — and to resort to every conceivable means to impede the growth of the true idea, which ascribes all power and glory to infinite Mind. Yet Religious Scientists, and students of Truth everywhere, must continue to (magnify only the good.) Good is thereby daily becoming to them more real, more tangible, more potent to bless and heal. These healings are natural manifestations of the ever-availability of Good. As we daily praise God, even for that good which is as yet unmanifest, we are hastening the day when the magnifying glass of praise will occupy the thoughts of all men and the whole world will catch the holy contagion. As Sir Thomas Browne said:

"Praise is a debt we owe to the virtues of others, and is due to our own, from whom malice has not made mutes or envy struck dumb."

* * *

In connection with this chapter, it might not be amiss to repeat here the meditation on page 43 of our book "Meditations," by Josephine Holmes Curtis, which is based on our "Questions and Answers" by Ernest Holmes and Alberta Smith.

"MY SENSE OF VALUES IS FREED FROM PERSONAL CONCERN."

Jealousy comes from a too confined concern with personal experience — seeing everything about me from a very limited viewpoint and re-acting very quickly as to how everything affects me personally. To be sure, I wish greater good, increased benefit, but it is not just by wishing them that they may be brought into being. It is by knowing and declaring forcefully that every-thing I do succeeds, that everything I think is vital, and that all my thoughts are creative.

It is by a firm proclamation of my innate, eternal Divinity, that the signs of Divinity fol-low in my experience. In a universal system so infinitely potential that the reaches of man's

53

thought can but feebly contemplate it, there is certainly a place for fantastic success on everyone's part. Therefore, what anyone has or does, does not rob or hinder me.

I wish good — great unlimited increased good —to everyone. Further than that, I *know* it for mankind. Then, as an overtone to this constant proclamation, I add this conviction: that my success and my experience of good and perfection are guaranteed to me right now! I allow myself to expand peacefully, and thankfully into the good which is for me.

CHAPTER III

"If I Were Only Younger!"

IF Walter Pitkin had written his splendid book, "Life Begins at Forty," fifty years ago, it would have been a great boon to this genera-tion. Nevertheless, we shall undoubtedly have, one of these days, a book with a title like "The Priceless Years After Seventy." Regardless of our attitude toward life, we are having to admit that the physical disabilities of age start, for the most part, with a mental attitude. When we persist in the realm of agitation and irritation, diseases begin to develop and what were once mental attitudes become functional disorders.

It is said that during the time that Oliver Wendell Holmes and Justice Brandies were on the Supreme Court Bench, they took a daily walk together. One afternoon, when Holmes was 92, the men passed an unusually attractive girl, and Holmes turned in frank admiration. Then to Brandies he murmured: "Ah! What wouldn't I give to be seventy again!"

Those of us around forty will chuckle at this
. . . the idea that *seventy* could even suggest
youth . . . yet Holmes is not the only man who
has been doing great things after ninety. We
should remind ourselves often of the great things
that have been accomplished by men after fifty,
rather than recall the remark made by Dr. Osler,
years ago, that men of forty had reached their
usefulness and should be chloroformed. The
world actually believed that for a time, in the
face of the fact that many great men have hardly
gotten into their stride until after fifty. It would
have been no small loss to the world if Abraham
Lincoln had not lived to be fifty, yet he had
achieved no notable victories prior to the time
he was elected President at the age of 51. Glad-
stone was elected Prime Minister to England
three times after his 60th birthday, and held office
until 85. William Cullen Bryant made his trans-
lation of the Iliad, one of his greatest literary
achievements, when he was in his seventies. The
records say that Socrates did not know one note
from the other when he was 75, and yet became
an accomplished musician before his death. Cato
began the study of Greek at 80. Joseph Conrad,
Milton, Alexander Dumas, Voltaire, and Bismark

were obscure figures at middle life, yet before their passing achieved glory which will be related to each succeeding generation.

These instances come readily to mind, without going into the historical cases of longevity, by which I could show you that numbers of people have led active lives long past the century mark, but these records are more than enough to prove that *youth* can be lived at least twenty-five or fifty years longer than we do ordinarily. For fear you may accuse me of dealing only with history, I must remind you of the marvelous come-back of Marie Dressler, a few years ago, when she was near seventy; of the new laurels of Mdme. Schuman-Heink at an even later age, and of Mrs. Patrick Campbell, at seventy, starting out to make a new fortune in the field of pictures, not to forget E. Phillips Oppenheim, 71, and still writing most exciting novels, and Maude Barger Wallach, former tennis champion, at 71 in Hollywood coaching Frank Shields on his tennis game. All of these are in our day.

Of course, you will understand I have no thought of going into the matter of *acquiring* youth or *preserving* youth. This is not the place to discuss the surgical rejuvenation as practiced by Lydston, Steinach, or Voronoff. None of the cases I have called to your mind come under such a head. The accomplishments of such men and women as I have called to your mind prove just one thing: Man is just as old as he thinks he is! Quoting Oliver Wendell Holmes again, (when he was asked how he preserved his vigor to such an age, he replied: "It is faith in something, enthusiasm for something, that makes life worth living.")

Certainly, we all desire to live life to its fullest. We feel, and rightly so, that living life abundantly will produce happiness, wisdom, health, plenty and peace. The barrier which blocks our desire is largely the inability to find out how life may be lived to the utmost. There is no sense in contradicting the evidence that thousands of people today are denied positions, which they are competent to fill, merely because they come under the classification of "old" or "middle-age." This is an experience we must recognize, but shall we not follow it almost simultaneously with the knowledge that this need not be manifested in our life?

We have discovered that many people have demonstrated perennial youth. The next question to determine, then, is it desirable? Is it right? Will it benefit us and the world? Since we know it is *possible*, if we know, also, that it is what God would have us do, then the only thing to do is to get busy on it. I think we all agree that the great ideas which are necessary to advance the world can only come from great minds, and these minds appear to be the product of years of experience which brings wisdom. So, for the betterment of the world, it would appear that youth *should* be maintained, so that our minds can unfold to greater perceptions of the infinite possibilities. That would seem to answer that part of our question.

Some of us are old at thirty and others are young at 90. It lies entirely within ourselves which it shall be. Formerly, we tried to pull ourselves together every seven years, having been taught that the body was made over every sev/ years, but now the scientists have proven t' our body is *completely new* in from three to el/ months — every cell, every muscle, gland, and bone made entirely new! Since God i/ ing anew the body every few months, i/ be that an old, decaying, withering /
serve the world better. We are forc/

conclude that God has given us eternal youth. We shall always be more than we now are, but there will never come a time when we shall get through being more than we are. It must be our deep conviction that no matter what age we are, we may look forward to the creativeness of our spirit, the eternal expansion of our own soul.

Just how old, then, would you be? When you are able to say to yourself, and truthfully, "I am never more than one year old," it seems that should be young enough for the best of us. It would be difficult for one to convince us of our lack of ability to fill any position, for which we had trained, on the ground that we were too old, if our consciousness were filled to overflowing with the positive fact that we never had been, are not now, and never can be, more than one year old! Can you not see, then, that a life filled with age-producing processes could not be in line with what God intended for us, and for this reason is a wrong conception of life. Does it not appear, then, that the age-producing habit is artificial, man-made?

With the illumination that comes to us from a study of Truth, we should have no trouble in beginning our transformation at once. If we are in our teens, let's retain our youth. If we have begun to think of old age and fear it, let's banish it forever from our thought. It would seem foolish, with a physical self that is new every year, for us to cling to antiquated mental habits that have held us in bondage — old prejudices, old envys, old grudges. You certainly must be aware, by this time, that(it is belief in anything that gives it form or manifestation.) If your thought is giving reality to a condition which you neither admire nor like, or for any reason do not wish to retain, can you not see that by withholding your impulsation of life from it, i.e., by changing your conviction of life about it, you will cause it to pass into oblivion? You have only to create new mental patterns for yourself and breathe into them the invigorating reality of life.

If you were twenty years old, according to the calendar, your body might be eleven months old. If you are fifty years old, your body is still between seven and eleven months old. Who shall say which gives forth a greater degree of reality, the fifty bodies you have discarded, which have gone back to their native substance, or the one which you are using at this moment. If you have improved your time, even slightly, there must be

an elasticity of the mind, a quickness of appre-
hension, a degree of livingness — real youth —
that you did not have at any previous year. It
seems impossible to let the thought of regret,
anxiety, or any negative thought that would rob
us, enter our consciousness, when we know the
body is never over one year old. We would be
ashamed to be seen going about our business,
with a dead body tied to our side, as if we were
the unsevered half of a deceased Siamese twin,
yet we are doing just that when we are perpetuat-
ing the emotions, the sorrows, the fancied wrongs
of our dead selves — the selves of yesterday —
rather than rejoicing in the vitalizing consciousness that we are today "joint heirs with Jesus
Christ," forever at the point of youthful perfection. Race memory has built up the idea of age
and experience. It is up to us to destroy this
effect of race memory. We, as sons of God, should
not be affected by race mind. We draw on Spiritual Substance for our supply. We do not draw
from a limited, finite reservoir of energy within
our particular bodies, but go directly to the
Source of all energy.

Then why the constant wail "If I were only
younger!" Is it because you would have a more

beautiful body, because you cannot feel a body fifty years old is attractive? We must not forget that attraction is a quality of Spirit. Is it because you would accomplish great things and you feel the time is too short? Is it that you would acquire wealth, and you believe this is the result of competitive effort, and you do not feel young enough to undertake it? Is it because you would be educated, and education is the work of eternity? Whatever it is, there is a way for you to build this new self — the spiritual self — as you could wish no younger *physical* body than you actually have . . . one year old. (*It is by giving to creative Mind the desires you would see manifested.*)Divine Intelligence within you is ever ready to co-operate with you in anything you would do.

All of us have seen tragedy, or sudden grief, seem to rob an individual of his conscious mind and years have passed without leaving the slightest impress, because the individual was unconscious of what we call the passing of time. Which is all the proof we need that any indication of age is the result of thought we have allowed to take root in our mind.

Many times we have parted with a friend and when we met him 24 hours later, he looked ten or twenty years older, because of some shock or great worry. Again this brings home to us that it is necessary that each new cell and fiber in our system be forever maintained by the vitalizing thought that we are eternally young. The chemical action of every cell in our body can be changed by the thoughts planted in subjective mind, where this chemical action has its root. But, no matter what method is employed, it will not be possible for man to perpetuate his youth *if he believes in the very depths of his being that age is inevitable!* It is absolutely imperative that the growing-old habit be eradicated from subjective mind.

But, let's remember one thing, we are not attempting to *produce youth.* If we were confronted with this staggering proposition, we might grow faint. YOUTH IS. It is only necessary for us to cease making the body feel and look old, when it is actually young. Looking at the faces all around us, lined with care and anxiety, it is an amazing fact to keep in mind that the man of eighty is just as young as the baby one year old! Just the same age.

We are not *trying to stay young.* This is so different from what we are attempting to tell you that it would produce the opposite result. In *trying* to stay young, we grow older each day, for we are acting on the premise that we are certain we are growing older and we must therefore try to do something about it. Thus, we are mentally accepting the belief that youth is escaping us, and we tie to our mentalities this misconception, and subjective mind, having nothing else to do but give us what we order, sends back to us a manifestation of diminishing youth.

Ernest Holmes remarked one Sunday that if it were possible, when a man came in with a broken back or leg, "we could just nonchalantly wave him into the next room, with the explanation 'Take him in there and the manufacturer will give him a new one', we would have no anxiety on that score." Subjectively, we have probably been thinking that when the Creator made us, He used all the Substance He had, and that when we should need a hew heart, new eyes, or new legs, there would be nothing out of which He could create such things. When, as a matter of fact, even physical science now makes the statement that the average person, who breathes properly, has about three pairs of new lungs each year; that the heart, the brain, and the nervous system, under average normal conditions, renew themselves every sixty or ninety days. The bony structure takes a little longer for the renewal process and requires from seven to fourteen months, while the skin is completely renewed every ten days or so!

But, as long as we believe we are growing older, and are watching year after year for the signs of age to appear, this mental attitude will cause the new cells to take on an old-age appearance, and the new body will look as old as we think it should.

We admit it takes a little more courage, a little more will power and understanding for the woman who feels she is past middle age, to enable her to drop an assured income, no matter how small and inadequate it is, and launch out into the field she feels certain she could make a success of, if it were not so late in life. The spirit of adventure and enthusiasm is not as strong at fifty as it was at twenty. But if a woman so situated could be made to realize that this idea of being older is no more real than last night's dream, would it not give her release?

The terrible curse of being always in a hurry, of rushing through life in a state of nervousness, comes from the belief that life is so short . . . youth so limited . . . and the time which we have, in which we can do things, is rushing by. So, the speed and confusion which we create, and attempt to live in, rob us of much of our power, unless we (remain poised at the center of our being.)

We attempt to use only one of our talents merely because we believe the time is too short in which to begin. If we know that we are eternally young, does this not inspire us to undertake that supreme achievement, for which we feel ourselves so fully equipped? When we free our minds from the thought that *time is passing*, we shall remain young. *Time is not passing: time is*, and the perpetual renewing process will prevent us from ever becoming more than one year old. If time does not pass, if it is merely a measure of man's experience, then man's life does not pass, youth does not pass! Fifty, sixty, seventy should be glorious mileposts, as the birthdays roll around: time for great rejoicing because of increased wisdom, but certainly a time free from any thought of decay, of declining power. When we gain this attitude of mind, we shall become so engrossed with the daily occupation,

67

everything else will be forgotten, as when we were in our teens.

I was in school with a woman who took up the study of French in her 80th year. She was with her granddaughter, but unwilling to waste the time, she put in four years of intensive study and the students of eighteen and twenty were kept busy trying to make grades as good as hers. She often said: "When you think years produce mental maturity, your growth will stop, and age then is inevitable, as decay always trails along after that which ceases to grow." And we must not forget that the great artist Titian was painting— and some thought more interestingly than at any period of his life — at 90. So, it is not surprising that the psychologist, Thorndyke, says that some men are at their best at forty and others are best at seventy. "The relationship between age and ability," he says, "is an individual thing. Some men at 89 come out as well in some tests as others at 45," which makes us say again, it is our own mental attitude which either prolongs youth or ends it.

Mr. Larson* says: "To him who has learned to stay young, the coming of more years means

*Christian D. Larson in "How To Stay Young."

68

the coming of more intelligence, more talent, more capacity, more usefulness, more real life, more real joy, more of everything that is rich and beautiful in the world. He does not dread the coming of years because to him it does not mean weakness, age, and empty idleness; instead it means youth, combined with experience; vigor combined with opportunity; visions of attainments combined with real attainments; desires combined with realization; the love of the rich and beautiful combined with the possession of the rich and beautiful; and the capacity to enjoy, combined with the possession of that which can give joy."

As many times as we have reiterated our statements, surely we shall not say again: "If I were only younger." We simply *couldn't* be any younger. We do not have to wait for perfection to appear — it is already inherent. We merely have to step out of the way with our old opinions and let Perfection express itself. *We must empty ourselves of all resistance to perfection!*

Why have we been thinking of ourselves as growing old, becoming more feeble, less alert? Why have we believed that dimmed vision, poor organic functioning, should take place in our physical being with the lapse of years? What is there about this Eternal Substance, out of which we are made, which shall decay in a few years? Could that which is the Source of our life with- draw from us bit by bit? Since God is not arbi- trary or comparative, He cannot know that He has endured more life in one man than in another. He could not be thought of as saying to Himself: "This man is aging, therefore, I must withdraw from him gradually." Undoubtedly, it must be that the idea of decay and depletion must be a limitation of man's thought. Let us, therefore, say to ourselves "God knows only now, and to- day there is just as much of the Infinite as in every other day, and as much for me. I drink deeply of that fountain of life, strength and vitality. Today I let this life force renew and rebuild my body after a pattern of perfection. My inspiration is from the Source of all good- ness, and never again will I say: 'If I were only younger'."

70

CHAPTER IV

Are You Mentally Weaned?

SO MANY students come to my classes, and many for private instruction, who seem to be grasping the truth of being, but they are not content because members of their family . . . a husband, a wife, a son, a daughter, a sister, an aunt, or someone whom they love . . . "needs this Truth so badly," and they are worried because the loved one will not manifest any interest in their explanation of it.

This is a perfectly natural, human reaction. We have a full appreciation of the fact that one always wishes to share every good thing with those one loves. And in our system of thought you will run no risk of being separated from those you love, by a deeper study of its principles. A study of Truth reveals a freedom for every individual, a new conception of the rights of every man, which brings about a closeness in the affections of families that has rarely been found elsewhere. This is appreciated by every member of the household, for as we gain understanding, we learn *not to try to change another.* We direct all our mental and spiritual powers toward harmony. We try to know that everyone connected with our home is unified and identified in love, understanding, wisdom and illumination, and everyone is expressing his part in the perfect Whole.

We do know, however, that it would be difficult to estimate the number of careers, even lives, ruined because of the demands made by relatives.

This is perhaps observed more often — at least it is more obvious to the casual observer — in the case of mother and child, either son or daughter. For this reason, most of our suggestion will be directed to the mother, hoping that she may *allow* her child to develop naturally, rather than to the child in an effort to show her how to sever the bonds . . . how to become *weaned.*

Sometimes this feeling of parental possessiveness is carried to such extremes that young married people are compelled to live in close proximity to the parents, whether it be the right place or not. Many times, we have known young husbands who have been forced to resign lucrative positions and move to a new town, in order to retain the wife's affection, because of some real or imagined claim of the girl's mother. This is an extreme condition, of course. Not a week passes, however, that we do not see the effect of some enforced influence.

Just recently, there came to my attention the case of a young woman whose relatives were preparing to have the necessary papers signed to place her in an institution for the insane. From listening to the reports from the parents, I might easily have believed that the young woman was suffering from "delusions." I might have credited their statements had I not been a metaphysician. When I saw the young woman, it was clearly evident to me that she was merely suffering from lack of expression. A college woman, of brilliant attainments, she was still required to pattern her life according to the ideas of close relatives, with the result that there arose in her such a rebellion, at not being allowed to think and act for herself; not being allowed to choose her own friends or decide upon her own occupation, that the force of her pent-up rebellion was almost ready to exterminate either herself or someone else. No wonder she acted "crazy-like."

73

Her first relief, after coming to our classes, came when she discovered that someone in the world *could* understand what was happening to her! Her amazement and gratitude were overwhelming. Then as the relatives were persuaded to treat her with consideration; as they were shown that the daughter is a perfect idea in the great Universal Harmony, and as such she is active, progressive, mentally alert and responsive; as they were urged to accept the fact that Divine Mind knows the daughter as an active, successful, progressive part of Itself, and that It compels her to think, say and do the right thing at the right time; then, and not until then, the tension was lifted and she returned home in a happy frame of mind, perfectly willing now to comply with most of their requests, being fortified with the knowledge that she was to be given her choice in the matter. She was to be allowed to discover herself, as an individual!

This is, in so sense a criticism of the parents. Certainly we would not impugn their motives, their loving solicitation for the welfare of their children. But, because they would shield their offspring from the hardships they, themselves, have endured, the result is, more often than not, that woman is doomed to a life of mental misery, because of not having been allowed to develop within herself self-reliance and independence. *Not mentally weaned.*

If you are fairly well satisfied with the results of your own life, you may ask, at this point, "Why should I not retain my influence over my child? Isn't she *my* child?" Which recalls to my mind an incident in the life of Robert Louis Stevenson, when he came upon a man beating a dog. Furious, he rushed in to stop the punishment, whereupon the man turned upon him: "He's my dog and I will beat him if I want to." "He's *not* your dog," said Stevenson, "He's God's dog and I am here to defend him."

But answering your question, you *will* influence your child, whether you wish to do so or not. But surely you would not want to limit her growth to the exact mold of your conception? She *might* be able to do even greater things than it is possible for you to imagine. How could any mother know better than God what a child's highest good is? Your problem is one of realizing that your daughter is an individual and must work out the evolution of her own soul. Every individual is a unique incarnation of the univer-

75

sal Spirit. Each has the same ultimate destiny, but all do not choose the same road. Instead of trying to coerce the will of your daughter, rather seek to realize that the Spirit within her is the directing force of her own life. Try to feel that she is being guided by an intelligent and perfect Mind. In so far as possible, relieve your own thought of personal responsibility and obligation in the matter, and you will have done two things; you will have relieved her mind of the suggestion of fear in your own thought . . . that she will not do the things you want her to do . . . and you will have opened up a channel of receptivity in her thought for the influx of intelligent and constructive guidance.

I like the illustration that Ruthanna Schenck uses, when she says: "Be certain that you want what you pray for." She uses as an illustration of the importance of this the story of a man hurrying home in his automobile, travelling along a little-used highway, where the mountain looms up immediately adjacent to the road on one side, and directly below the road on the other side a deep ravine, hundreds of feet deep, making the path of safety "steep and narrow." Suddenly, he is aware that another car is approaching him, and at only one point on the road is there room to pass another car. The wide stretch in the road is only a few hundred feet away, but the speed of the other car makes it seem to the man that inevitable destruction is bearing down upon him. He prays earnestly: "Oh, God, *do* let me make the wide space in the road," and simultaneously he applies all the power he has in his car and reaches the wide space just as the other car rushes by. But, before he can express his relief, he feels the ground crumbling beneath him, and his car is plunged to destruction below. He had come upon a "soft shoulder" in the road and it had given way beneath the weight of his car.

That man, as you can readily see, outlined how his protection should come . . . by reaching the wide space in the road. When he first saw the other car, had he been able to realize that he was in God's hands, as well as was the man in the other car, and had he wanted only the greatest good to them both, i.e., "Thy will be done," God could have taken care of him in a far better manner. His prayer *was* answered: he reached the wide place in the road.

Such outlining, or any outlining, no matter how great and comprehensive to human sense it appears, is working in limitation. It is not our business to outline. That is God's business. Our business is to specifically set the law of right action in motion (whether this be for ourselves or our children). A right attitude is one that believes there is but One Mind, and that this Mind knows exactly what to do and how to do it; and that *it does it at the bidding of your spoken word;* that it opens the best channels, using the most powerful agencies, human and divine, for the accomplishment of your desire. Doesn't this take a great load of responsibility from your shoulders?

I do so wish, my friends, that I could make you understand that this mental weaning is no less important than that the child, in infancy, be weaned from its mother's milk at the proper time. By this we would not intimate that there should be less respect or love for the parent, but that as the young man (or young woman) grows, at the proper stage of his development, *not only should he be allowed to think and act for himself, but he should be compelled to do so!*

We might take a valuable lesson from the mother bird, whose instinct for the protection of her young will brook no interference as she

78

sits on the eggs awaiting the arrival of her little ones. When approached, she recognizes no adversary too immense for her to combat — either man or beast. If the lives of her young are imperiled, she is totally oblivious of any danger which might threaten her in the combat. Yet, when these birds are a certain number of days old, if they show no inclination to find out about the world around them; if they make no attempt to fly, she gently *pushes* them out of the nest. Perhaps first on the limb of a tree, then if they do not hop further of their own accord, she noses them off into the air. The necessity arouses the latent instincts in them, and *they fly*. Did she not do this, her little birds would be the helpless prey of every passing marauder.

Just so with us. If we are not disciplined at the various stages of our growth, life disciplines us later, and many of us are not sufficiently prepared to meet the onslaught. Some people are so far from being awake on this point, that they would guide their children throughout life, as is proven by the terms of too many "last wills and testaments."

This allowing your child to stand alone, mentally, may not seem so terribly important to you, but it is. And any problem that touches our lives is a problem to be met in Truth. If we can permit our souls to wait in silence for God only, every expectation will be fulfilled in Him. The hand of God is not shortened. The omnipotent, omnipresent, and omniscient Presence is right where your child is. If Omniscience cannot lead him or her aright, it would be useless for you to try to do so. As you are lifted up, so you draw your children (and all children) into the realm of perfect realization and manifestation. Sometimes the good *we* plan for our children is only a tiny speck, as compared to the good that God has in store for them.

If we desire for our children the greatest happiness in the world — and who does not — if we wish for them a degree of prosperity that will at least insure a fair amount of what we call "the good things of life"; if we wish for them an intellectual attainment that will merit the respect and admiration of their associates, there IS a way this can be done. It is by knowing within ourselves that our child is really not our child, but the child of Perfect Life, under a Perfect Law, and performing or manifesting in Perfect Action. It is by knowing that our boy or girl is

God's perfect child—whole, sound, perfect, complete, and that he is sustained, inspired, guided and directed by the One Infinite Mind, God.

However, we shall never be able to insure them this degree of happiness by exacting any promise of any kind from them; and not by tying them to our apron strings, so that they will never be able to function in the world without "coddling" from some one. Not by preaching either "don'ts" or "dos" can this be achieved, but only by showing them that every conscious moment of our lives we not only have access to Omniscience, but that we avail ourselves of it. If we consciously turn toward the omnipresent light of His Spirit— pure radiance of divine love, the effulgent light of divine grace and faith—there will be no doubt in the minds of our children. They will know that we are lifting up the light of an unquenchable faith, a shining torch of Truth, that will allay every doubt.

They will see we are directed to successful achievement of good; that by His wisdom and strength all of our duties are accomplished easily, happily and in order. As we allow God to fill our lives, to guide and direct our children, our mode of living and serving will expand to meet

His standard for us. And what child would ever be separated from this? There could be found no greater magnet in all the world to draw them to you, nor could their lasting interest be aroused in anything half so important. We cannot force any human being to live according to our standards, whether it be our child, our neighbor's child, or our grandchild. Nor should they, perhaps, because they are all at a different stage of growth, but we can help every individual whose life touches ours by our mental attitude toward him—by seeing only perfection in him, and leaving it free to come into manifestation.

One thought we must cling steadfastly to; there is a harmonious solution for every problem, and if we know this and co-operate with the law, we can bring harmony out of any chaotic condition. If our children see things differently from us, they are often equally sincere, and they may only be seeing things from a different angle. For instance, the gate to Mary Pickford's estate, "Pickfair," usually stands wide open, and one passing the road on that side can get a beautiful view of the house, the gently sloping green lawn, and the swimming pool at the far end. Someone looking through a small aperture in the fence on the other side, would see clumps of rare shrub-bery, with flowers nestling here and there, but they would likely not be able to see the house at all. Both views would be correct. Is the child to be blamed if he is viewing it only from the peephole? His vision is right for him, but we should keep our eyes on the larger vision and not struggle with the boy, lest we force him to tram-ple under foot the modest flowers growing near by. In his own time, he will wander around and get the wider view. There is no reality in any-thing but God, and what each one of us sees is but a different manifestation of the One and only Power. The service that Christ would perform in us and through us does not interfere with the services of others or deplete or restrict one life to enrich another.

Maturity, in the best sense of the term, should mean that adult young people are permitted to get away from parental ties *emotionally*, to the extent of being able to decide for themselves all matters which make for lasting happiness. A man should be competent to choose his life's mate—though many times from never having been allowed to stand on his own judgment and initiative, he is not. It should certainly mean that he should be allowed to attend to his business duties without having to be "coddled" by a superior officer.

Few pictures are more pathetic than that of the young man who spends half his time seeking advice from others, *because he has never been mentally weaned from his parents.* Too long he has been sheltered, guided, even to being told what clothes to wear; when too cold or too hot; when to stay home and when to go out; what to read and what to leave alone. If perchance he does make a mistake then, when following such exact instructions, his tendency is to throw the responsibility on his parents—a natural reaction. This is why so often we find college boys leaving hotel bills to be paid by "Dad"; getting into scrapes and trusting to parental power to straighten it out, showing that he has never been able to view the world outside of his immediate family circle. Subjectively, he believes that his father can fix everything.

If, instead of this condition, the boy had been given an understanding of his real parentage; of God as the loving Father, verily he *could* have depended on Him to fix everything. However, a life modeled after this pattern would never be found in the position of the first boy. To be sure, there would be difficulties, as in every life, but if the boy is made to realize that he is God individualized, and that no human being can ever do his work for him; that *whatever his work is, it is just as important to God as the work of any other man in the universe,* can't you see how this would raise him in his own estimation, filling him with joyous, bouyant confidence? In addition, the boy should be given the understanding, in the clearest manner possible, that *no man has any work in the world but the work of expressing God,* and this can be done in the factory, in the school, behind a counter, in a bank, or on a farm. Any work that man finds himself doing can be done to the glory of God; and *only by each man doing his own work, in the perfection which God reveals to him,* can the mosaic of life be kept in all its pristine beauty, with God the Master Artist, viewing each mite of humanity in its proper place, and the whole as Good.

* * *

The thoughts in this chapter bring to my mind an instance of where a young woman was never emotionally and mentally weaned from the impressions of her childhood; and her lack of expression was so complete that it almost ruined several lives. If the reading of this will help someone avoid a similar mistake, it will be well worth my telling the details.

In one of my classes last year, I noticed a woman who kept a handkerchief wound about her hands most of the time. When questioned about the cause, she explained that she was afflicted with Eczema, and had been, almost continuously, for about fifteen years; that she had to do her own housework, washing dishes, washing and ironing clothes, and when the hands were exposed to soap and water in this manner, they cracked open and were excrutiatingly painful. In addition, she had a goiter, for which the surgeons and physicians could do nothing. This was the surface condition.

The woman was questioned at great length. (You may recall that Phineas P. Quimby, one of the first men ever to recognize the power of thought, in trying to explain his healings, said it was the *explanations* which did it. This is true as far as it goes.)

When this woman was born, she had a sister slightly older than herself, and her father died when she was quite small. The mother was compelled to manage as best she could and the dresses of the older child were naturally passed on to the younger one. As the years passed, the mother turned, in companionable fashion, and talked with the older girl as soon as she could comprehend. So, there gradually formed in the mind of the younger child that the sister was the recipient of the mother's confidences, had better clothes, etc., *by some divine right, some innate superiority,* and it produced in the younger girl a terrific inferiority complex. She was only able to go through High School and soon after married a college man, with whom she had fallen deeply in love. When she met the boy's mother, one of the first questions she asked was "Did you go to college?" and upon learning that the new daughter-in-law was only a High School graduate, she exclaimed: "Now, my son can never amount to anything!"

It seems that this mother, through almost unbelievable vicissitudes, had just been able to put her boy through college, believing that a college degree was an open sesame to the world's treasures and that *a person cheated of this could never amount to anything.* It was no pose with the woman, but a burdensome fact. The young wife, then and there, developing an even greater in-feriority complex, made up her mind *that never in her entire life would she say anything that would prevent this man's wisdom from having full sway.* And she kept her word. IN THE SEVENTEEN YEARS SHE HAD BEEN MARRIED TO HIM, SHE HAD NEVER EXPRESSED AN OPINION! As her two children grew up (one of them now in High School) they came with vari-ous questions and requests, to all of which she gave the same response: "Ask your father." She was wholly unexpressed and the husband was beginning to wonder what was the matter. He could never be certain he was pleasing her. He knew nothing of what transpired between his mother and his wife, sixteen years before, as SHE HAD NEVER BREATHED IT TO A SOUL!

When asked how long she had suffered from the Eczema, she replied, fifteen years or so. "And how long since the conversation with your moth-er-in-law?" "Perhaps sixteen years," she an-swered.

"How do you feel when you think of your mother-in-law?" she was asked.

"I always have a fearful sense of irritation,"

and then as she seemed to recognize that she had answered her own question, she exclaimed, "COULD that be it?"

Having opened her eyes to that much, the problem now became how to undo this. She was then asked: "If you had made great plans, as well as great sacrifices for your boy, expecting that he would certainly make his mark in the world, and then some woman came along and wrapped him around her finger, someone whom you thought wholly unworthy of him, what would be your reaction to it?"

"I think I could kill her," she replied.

"Then you will at least be able to *understand* how your husband's mother felt about you (when the lack of a college education was so vital a thing to her) no matter how worthy you really are?"

"Yes, I think I do," she said slowly.

"That's good. If you can *understand* how she could say those things, then you can forgive her," and she nodded her head.

Without waiting for her to recover her surprise, she was asked how she felt every time she felt sorry for herself, all through the years when she had no one to talk with, and she explained that she always felt a tightening, choking of the throat. The goiter! In two weeks' time, the hands were perfectly healed, and the goiter disappeared in less time.

In this case, the woman was unexpressed because of life-long inhibitions — inferiority complexes. The physical discomfort was the sole result of her smoldering resentment against her mother-in-law, combined with her self-pity. The explanation lifted her into complete freedom.

CHAPTER V

"Rightly Dividing the Word . . . "

TENNYSON at the close of his life, it is said, remarked to a friend: "My chief desire is to have a new vision of God." This is what the world desires today: A new vision of God!

It must have been a similar longing which prompted Emerson, in 1883, to ask in his Divinity School Address, "Why should *we* not have a first-hand and immediate experience of God?" Men are still asking "Why should we not have our *own* experience and not have to depend solely upon the experience of others?" "Are we further removed from our Creator than the men of ancient days, that we cannot contact Him?"

How grateful we are that Jesus answered all these question so completely. He made it plain that it is possible for every man to attain his deeper knowledge of God *through his own consciousness:* "The things that I do shall ye do also, and greater things, because I go unto the Father."

Religious Science stands preeminently for healing, and man is looking to this great movement expecting practical results. If we would prove its highest usefulness, so that it will, indeed, be "a city set on a hill," we need to strive for an understanding heart, that mankind will sense a genuine, impartial love so permeating us that we shall have nothing less to give to the world. There should be constant vigilance that "evil does not insinuate itself as good; that it does not tempt us as attractive, and that it does not frighten us as powerful."

But to those who have devoted themselves unavailingly to material means for healing, the teachings and claims of Religious Science are foreign to past experience, and to some appear quite incomprehensible. The inquiries are increasingly insistent, "How does Religious Science heal?" "What does it claim for itself?" "What are its limitations?" "Who is qualified to practice this healing, and to what extent has its efficacy been proven?" This is a large order, but we shall be able to satisfactorily answer anyone who is conscientiously seeking the good which this teaching bestows, for Mind is omnipresent.

Marcel Proust once said, in a talk to writers,

that anyone "who has several times contented himself with expressing his thought in an approximately pleasing way, has once and for all set a boundary to his talent, and will never pass beyond." If this is true of writers, it is much more true of teachers and practitioners, for nothing could be more disastrous than to undertake mental and spiritual healing while yet thinking in a careless manner. By *practitioner*, I mean any person who grasps the fact that(thought is creative, and determines to better his or her condition by the use of this knowledge.)

Above all things, we must not merely express our thoughts in an *"approximately pleasing"* way. Our basic facts must be correct. If our thought develops from a shifting foundation, the first wind of criticism will blow our conclusions far and wide. We must, therefore, build our premise on the Absolute, even if we are compelled to speak much in the relative. If we can plainly and simply state the Truth and, what is better, prove by the results of our application that we have understood it, we will not need to scream our message from the housetop. Men will beat a path to our door to listen. As Edith Wharton once said:

"It is useless to box your hearers' ears unless you have a Salamander to show them. (If the heart of your little blaze is not animated by a living, moving Something, no shouting or shaking will fix your story in your hearers' memory.) The Salamander stands for the fundamental significance that made the story worth telling."

That we do have a *Salamander* in Religious Science is proved by the multiplied and unsurpassed healings, these coming in an ever-increasing ratio!

With Spinoza, we say: "Some begin from created things, and some from the human mind. I begin from God." Perfect God, perfect man and perfect universe: this is our premise. Because of this all-encompassing Truth, Religious Science assures us that there is no condition, however deep-seated or serious it may appear, which cannot be reached, remedied and healed. No longer do we need to look upon the Scriptural healings as beautiful but uncertain stories or myths. Now we are able to read the prophecies, promises and proofs, in which the Scriptures abound, and realize that these signs and wonders are not mere miracles belonging to a previous age, but are illustrations of an ever-present, divine Law, and

94

are capable of attainment in all ages. It has been proven that God's law, rightly understood, will antidote every phase of discord or discomfort which might assail the individual — removing all sense of need or incapacity because it would remove all sense of separation from God. Religious Science is proving the allness of God, Good, by demonstrations rather than by words and arguments.

In order to enlarge our conception of God, there has been introduced into our teachings synonyms of God, other than those commonly used: First Cause, Creator, the Great I Am, The Unborn One, the Uncreated, the Absolute or Unconditioned, the One and Only, Mind, Love, Life, Truth, Intelligence, Substance . . . all indications of His nature, attributes or qualities. The proper conception of these terms lifts us out of any circumscribed, limited, or humanized sense of Deity, and directs us to the thought of Supreme Presence and Power — God.

Religious Science further holds that it is just as important for us to understand perfect man as the manifestation of God, as it is for us to have a true knowledge of perfect God as the creator of man.

95

"Because we are self-conscious and know our-selves, we are positive that God — the one In-finite Life — must know Himself, as we could not possibly be more than the Life from which we came and in which we have our being. God, being all there is, cannot feel or know lack of any kind, nor the possibilities of lack, for He has within Himself that which meets every thought, and even God could not imagine or think of some-thing which could not be. The Infinite is com-pletely existent at every point within It. But the Infinite has many attributes which co-exist throughout the universe, and we are but aspects of the One Being, which exists in and through all things. These Divine qualities are present in infinite measure at every point.

"Each being, each life, whether high or low in the scale of consciousness or evolution, ex-presses and experiences these perfect attributes of health, happiness, beauty, harmony, abund-ance, (only to the extent of that Being's knowledge of their existence within it. Man possesses all the qualities of God, but experiences them only as he awakens to their presence within him.) The Real Man needs nothing, is forever perfect, needs nothing outside of his own Divine Nature for complete satisfaction and complete expression. *But, the man that appears, becomes the man that is, only as this Divinity is sensed and understood. Man's entire future, all that he will ever experience, is within him now* " (Science of Mind Magazine.) Thus does Religious Science convey its high conception of both God and man. This teaching, revealing the Oneness of Mind, is today enabling many a student to subdue the beginnings of discord and disease before they rear themselves into towers of confusion.

With the completeness of all these statements about the Perfection and Infinity of God, is our attitude toward evil, lack and limitation clear? The statement that we make that God is the *only* Power, would seem to eliminate evil, but it is tremendously important that there be no doubt in your mind about this, for "*if evil is a power, it is necessarily a part of the eternal government of the universe and no mortal could ever hope to escape from it.*" We must have the proper concept of God before we can serve Him aright. Is He the One and Only Power, or must we recognize the power of evil as opposed to Him? The whole tenor of the Bible is that man does *not* worship God acceptably, while he is believing in both good and evil. If one is to be at peace, he must know the truth about God and this truth must actuate his every thought and act.

To concede the existence of *any* other power is surely to deny the omnipotence of God; but we have been able to prove the power of Good by obeying It, so to us the powerlessness of evil becomes evident. It is laughable — at least, inconsistent — the manner in which we condemn atheists for their disbelief in the existence of God, and yet we who call ourselves Christians (thereby acknowledging God as Infinite) go right on, half our time, believing in evil, the supposed opposite of God!

The First Commandment, which is certainly as much in force today as it was hundreds of years ago, was not given for practitioners alone; it requires that all men keep God first in everything, which clearly means that we are to know no other power than God . . . no other power than Good. And not a single command of the Bible demands the recognition of evil as a power or reality, but rather is evil condemned, and man exhorted to turn from it and find happiness and life. If God is literally and absolutely the only power, the only Creator and Governor of the universe, then it means that God is all, and nothing contrary to the nature of God — disease, want, pain, and death — has been created, set in operation, or permitted by Infinite Wisdom; that there is no truth or life in any of these wrong conditions; that they never had and never can have any power; that they cannot touch and never have touched the Real Man. It means that we have no reason to fear or obey evil in any form, but rather have we the authority of Jesus to reject it. It has been proven that evil has no actuality outside of the consciousness that believes it, and reliance upon the Infinite power of God, in the face of all physical testimony to the contrary, has delivered thousands from suffering, thereby demonstrating the verity of Jesus' teachings and the possibility of following his example.

I have repeated my statements that you may be certain that Religious Science recognizes only One Power and that Power Good; only One Force operating in all the activities of humanity and that Force, God. And its claims are that there is no need which human beings can experience which cannot be met by Omnipotence. And the method by which this is done is by RIGHT THINKING.

Then what is required of a teacher or practitioner? How much of average living must be eliminated if one would practice this Truth? Is there a technique which must be acquired before this work can be done? These and many allied questions must be answered. We can do no better than refer to the textbook used by Religious Scientists, the *Science of Mind*, in which Dean Holmes says:

"The whole basis of the possibility of mental healing rests upon the premise that (we all live in One Creative Mind, which reacts to our belief) To daily see the perfect man and to daily declare for his objective appearance is correct mental practice and will heal."

And a little further on, we read ("*Anyone can heal who believes that he can, and who will take time to put that belief in motion through the Law.*" And "we can demonstrate to the level of our ability to know, but beyond this we cannot go . . . When there is no longer anything in our mentality that denies our word, demonstration will be made."

Does this sound simple, or is it so simple that it confuses? The experience of many people proves that they have not understood. And

Richard Ingalese reports that he had thousands of letters from people who, hearing of the power of mind for the first time, decided they would not work any more. They would merely determine for themselves just what they wanted and wait until it came. You do not need to be told the result. We are sorry to relate that people have attended our classes, and "seeing as through a glass darkly" have eagerly grasped the thoughts of freedom and abundance held out to them, without gaining any conception of the truth that even God cannot do for them more than He can do through them. They have been heard to remark "I know I am going to have that car. I have been able to visualize it perfectly" . . . "I know my new home is waiting for me. I am already looking for furniture," and so on, with the result that demonstrations not being made at once, these individuals were convinced that the Principle had failed them. Electricity is wonderful when we use it according to the laws governing it, but when we refuse to do so, we can be electrocuted instantly by the handling of a "live wire."

You must see that we have not read comprehendingly the line " . . . who will take time to put that belief in motion *through the law.*" Nor have we understood the next line: "We can demonstrate to the level of our ability to *know.*" It must be borne in mind that *we cannot know a thing which is not true.* Therefore, what we have to know about this business of healing is the Truth of being: the truth of the Oneness and Allness of God and man's unity with It, then " . . . (when there is no longer anything in our mentality that denies our word, demonstration will be made.') Thus, we can readily see, with the understanding that man is forever sustained, supplied in and by Mind, our word cannot declare for him anything other than perfect health, perfect happiness, complete abundance. (When there is nothing in our consciousness to deny this, when we have the mental equivalent of the thing we want, there is no power in heaven or earth which can keep this from manifesting.)

We are happy that our system of thought is not meant to prepare humanity for a heaven to be reached at some future date; its teachings are intended to meet the demands of today. It is *now* that men need to be healed of disease and sin; and it is even now, as they are healed through this understanding of Mind, that they enter heaven! Paul must have known that he was enunciating the operation of the law of divine Principle, when he said "Be ye transformed by the renewing of your minds." This, we take it, means that Truth, operating in our consciousness, will overturn whatever is not of God until nothing shall remain that can delude or disturb mankind.

We are taught that personal magnetism has nothing to do with healing; that we have no personal responsibility for the healing, meaning that *we do not have to make this power work.* We are merely to direct this Power and let It work. Neither do we "hold a thought" for anyone, as some people suppose. We *release* thought. We neither attempt to suggest to, hypnotize, or mentally influence anyone. We simply know that man is forever a spiritual being, and through this knowledge, we set in motion the law that must bring this perfection into objective manifestation. "If your own thought is clear, you are able to completely realize the Presence of Spirit in your patient, and all the power on earth cannot hinder you from healing."

This must not lead us to the conclusion that

there *is* no responsibility in the matter of healing through the principles taught in Religious Science. Success in demonstrating the operation of spiritual law is always proportional to man's spiritual understanding; and spiritual understanding depends on the attainment of "that mind which was in Christ Jesus." So we do have the responsibility of right thinking. As some one has said, "Daily, spiritual work is of incalculable value — refining, purifying, tempering. Each day's tempering leaves the steel of true thought more potent, more perfect, more pure." And a further study of our textbook shows us that this is exactly what Dean Holmes has in mind, for he gives the further instruction:

"If you know that the Power with which you are dealing is Principle and not personality; if you know and believe that Mind is the only Actor, Cause, Effect, Substance, Intelligence, Truth, and Power there is; and if you have a real embodiment of your desires, then you can demonstrate.) . . . A good treatment is always filled with the recognition of the Presence of God or Good. Even in spiritual things, we are dealing with cause and effect, for God is Law. *The more exalted the thought, the more heavenly, the more boundless, (the more Godlike or Christlike the thought, the more power it will have."*)

It is a natural conclusion, that in order to accomplish the healing of Christ, as Jesus did, (one must be thinking in a Christlike or Godlike manner.) Jesus taught that eternal life is coincident with the knowledge of God, and of the Christ, which he so fully manifested; and he further taught that the only thing to which man is subject is to God's supreme law of eternal harmony. So, it should be obvious, it seems to me, that each time our thinking reaches a degree of Christlikeness, it should correct or heal any seeming lack or discord, for we have clearly apprehended that this consciousness of God is a law of elimination and obliteration to anything unlike Itself. How clearly manifest it becomes that our negative thinking must be progressively eradicated!

Even when knowing that man is kept by divine Love in uncontested security, by the comforting fact that there is only one Mind, what does a practitioner do when he gets up some morning with a feeling of depression or a headache, or some inexplicable feeling, which makes him ask whether or not he should take a case that day —even makes him wonder if he ever could heal

anyone or anything . . . just what does a practitioner do then? You are astounded that a
practitioner or teacher ever has such a period?
You must bear in mind that even Jesus was
tempted and practitioners cannot hope to escape
from the assaults of the enemy. Even with those
who are classed as spiritually-minded men and
women, feeling and sense emotion have much to
do with their faith and habits. Yet all of us
know that these states of *feeling* do not cancel
our ability to think correctly, to know the verity
and immutability of divine laws, which we know
we understand and have repeatedly proved.

So, what do we do? Does a temporary sense of
depression, discouragement or discomfort, alter
in any manner our ability to use the multiplica-
tion table? If we were called on to make change
for our newsboy, no matter how depressed we
were, we still would likely know that 50c from
$1.00 leaves 50c. So what does a feeling of dis-
comfort have to do with our ability to declare
effectively the healing word of Truth. Isn't this
one of our greatest blessings — that we can have
a clear perception of divine law and its unfailing
operation, regardless of any disabling sense feeling? The *knowing* life is one of peace and poise

and progress. (The life that is governed by feeling must ever be one of impulse and instability.) So, we can never escape the duty that faces us, merely because we don't "feel up to par." (Feeling has nothing to do with knowledge.) Demonstrable knowledge of the Truth is our one reliable and satisfying possession.

It would be a silly and impossible undertaking, either as teacher or practitioner, if we did not know that the laws we use are unchangeable, "The same yesterday, today, and forever," and that *what we think about them; whom we think should benefit by them*, have nothing to do with the operation of these laws. This knowledge is our rock and our fortress. God's law is intelligent and harmonious in its activity and this law controls all in perfect harmony throughout creation.

(In the 23rd chapter of Matthew, we read "Cleanse first the inside of the cup and of the platter, that the outside thereof may become clean also.") There are some of us whose minds need to be cleaned of one thing and other minds need to be freed from something else. Each will know his own work, but if we watch ourselves carefully, we shall be able to see here and there

the thoughts which, if eliminated, would further
the coming into expression of Christ through us.
The fidelity to God, which requires that our
minds be kept free from everything unlike Him,
so that every minute of existence they are receptive to Him, *is not an easy thing*, because we
are yet buried in the thoughts of the human race,
the problems around us, and the misery crying
out to us.

At this point, may I remind you that Religious
Scientists, who would progress, must be willing
to forget as well as to remember. The gracious
art of forgetting things harmful is not to be acquired by any power of the will nor any pre-
scribed regimen. If it is not inherent in the
natural faculty of our memory, then it must be
infused by the alchemy of Religious Science.
Many times we hear the remark: "I can forgive
but I cannot forget." With our knowledge —
our effort to become mentally one with goodness
and mercy — we know there can be no true
forgiveness without ready forgetfulness, the two
being coordinate and inseparable. The offense
must be wiped out of thought if the forgiveness
is to be complete. Since we have learned the
falsity of discord and evil, demonstrating that

only good is actual, we are able to expunge from memory such parts of our experience as appear evil. Thus we free ourselves of much worry and disappointment that would fasten upon us.

When it seems that we are unable to demonstrate that which we started out to demonstrate, we must not allow ourselves to become confused. It is right here that we need to think clearly. Our apparent failure is no indication that our "system" has failed. *When the good which we desired — whether for ourselves or for others — is not manifest, it is not that God is at that moment less than God.* He is giving all, just as He always has. This good, however, is never available to us if we do not perceive and utilize it. How can we perceive it if we are bearing a secret grudge against our neighbor; when we covet the new house being erected on our street; when we are annoyed that the practitioner in the next block has more patients than we? How can the light of spiritual Truth illumine our way, and the way of those who come to us for guidance, if such "smudge-pots" of selfish desire have clouded the rays? Infinite Mind has no knowledge of selfishness, greed, or ill-will and as such qualities are not attributes of the One Mind, they do not belong to us.

Some one has asked the question: "How many hours a day are we supposed to give to this work, if we are professional practitioners?" The question itself implies a gross misunderstanding of that which we have undertaken. It is imperative that we understand that God is not just working with us when we are "knowing the Truth," but that He is "active in season and out of season." The query might suggest that a portion of our time the truth about God was known to us, and perhaps the other portion, our eyes were not focussed on the Oneness in which all good is included — like a business partner who might leave us for half the time to carry the responsibility of our business alone. *We never work alone.* We must understand that God is forever blessing us. We must disabuse our minds of the thought that God is blessing us at only certain times of the day; that He listens only when we ask for an audience.

God is always omnipresent peace, harmony, right action, spiritual substance — NOT JUST WHEN WE REMIND HIM THAT HE IS! True, we have greater realizations of this at some periods of meditation than others. These moments should serve as inspiration to lift our thought when we seem to be running in "low gear." We should constantly be as conscious of our unity with God, as we are that we are breathing. "Closer is He than breathing, nearer than hands and feet."

When this has taken hold of both our conscious and our subjective mind, we shall know, if money appears to be our need, what we actually need is to recognize the omnipresence of spiritual abundance. If we think we need more friends, we shall remember the Friend "who sticketh closer than a brother." Our business is only to become conscious of our oneness with this blessing. God's law exists, and we apply It according to the measure of our understanding. "With all thy getting, get understanding." Recognition of God as the source of all good; faith in His good and gratitude for the blessings received; definite desire through spiritual illumination, belief in the certainty of fulfillment, and a continuous attitude of joy and praise — when these elements are present, demonstration is sure. How many hours each day do we give to knowing this? EVERY MINUTE OF OUR EXISTENCE!

As some one has said: "It is a great privilege to be divinely accredited to leadership, to be entrusted with the emblem of power and ability, and to use it 'rightly dividing the word of truth', before whose liberating advance the inanimate is quickened and the fearful and wavering made strong and steadfast. However, it is a far more wonderful gift to be so taught of God that one's inmost thoughts are so purified that no seed of self-love can ever find lodgment."

The highest form of healing is in the absolute spiritual realization, and as man partakes of the Divine nature of God, he unifies himself with his indwelling Christ. Thus does man approach this indwelling Presence, guided and governed by Divine Love. Thus does man feel that he is heeding the injunction given in Second Timothy, 2:15:

"Study to shew thyself approved unto God, a workman that needeth not to be ashamed, rightly dividing the word of truth."

CHAPTER VI

The Illusion of Progress

BEFORE I begin this discussion, I think I should preface my remarks by the statement that I believe in progress. I believe in prosperity, in abundance — even in opulence. You will find, I think, that all people associated with the New Thought movement, whether they be Religious Scientists, Christian Scientists, Divine Scientists, Unity Students, or members of some other branch of Truth, enjoy a greater degree of what we term "creature comforts" than perhaps any other class of people which can be found.

It is not at all unlikely, however, that we may differ on our definition of the word *progress*. While in the minds of most of us the words progress, success, prosperity, and happiness are used interchangeably, to the point of our accepting them as synonomous terms, if now, at the outset of this discussion, we can determine the actual meaning of the word *progress*, we shall have fewer

113

misunderstandings. Progress, so the dictionary informs us, comes from two words: *pro*, meaning forward, and *gradi*, meaning to step, hence the idea of progress being *a going forward;* a proceeding onward, as from one point or degree *to one further advanced.* As long as it is possible for us to measure our steps by this rule, whether the progress be physical, financial, mental or spiritual, we shall know just where we stand.

As I heard a prominent minister in New York say: "All of us must see that whatever else is true about progress, it is no escalator, no smoothly-flowing river; it is a spiritual achievement, a hard way, easy to lose anywhere — in a family, in a personality, in a civilization," and his further comment on it was that *the swiftest way to lose it is to be fooled by the illusion of it!*

(Whether we speak of prosperity, success or progress, what we really have in mind is happiness.) It is happiness that we are hoping to arrive at. Whatever our seeming lack of the moment, our thought is that a generous supply of that particular commodity would bring us happiness. History does not prove that this is so. If right now we believe that we are handicapped by the lack of money, invariably we feel that an abundance

114

of money would make us superlatively happy. If it does, that is good. But does this always follow? How many families have you seen pass through every type of privation, making unbelievable sacrifices for one another, and held together by strongest ties of devotion, only to have all their harmony dissipated on the rock of prosperity?

This is not to discourage you against the acquisition of money, but it is to stimulate your memory to the consciousness that when we attract money, for money's sake alone, it is no part of real progress. What I am trying to say is that progress is a much wider thing than we commonly assume; it is broader than the process of making money, which is the standard by which we have allowed the world to judge progress. The entire substance of progress must be found in the degree to which we struggle upward. The more widely in character and sympathy we are able to expand, the better we shall meet all the tests of progress.

How can we tell whether our ideas of progress are true? How can we tell whether our money is controlling us or we are controlling it? If it is interfering with our peace of mind, then, decidedly, it is controlling us. Someone has suggested a good test on the subject of "possessions," is to ask yourself, "Could I do without them?" If you find you could be happy without them, then you are safe in keeping them. Robert Louis Stevenson must have had a fine understanding of this when he wired his congratulations to a friend whose house had just burned. Another writer gives a helpful suggestion in this connection. When tempted to acquire more *things*, she stops and says to herself: "*Things* have to be dusted. Can I spare the time?"

It is important, too, in our zeal to get money, that we do not forget *why* we wanted it, just as in your childhood days you clutched so tightly the dime that had been given you to buy bread that when you reached the grocery store you could not think what you had come after. "When my ship comes in, I am going to give 20% to the Lord," we hear someone say. Later, when riches have been accumulated, even the 10% which had previously been given is forgotten. Was that *progress*, or might it not better be called retrogression? Of course, we know that the *real man* does not retrogress, for he cannot. He is forever unfolding at the point of perfection. Even in the universe around us, and in the physical life of man, the natural law of growth is continual, unless there is interference with it. In other words, if our conscious minds have never entertained a negative thought of poverty, we would automatically attract prosperity, *growth being nature's first law.*

In trying to arrive at what is true and what is false, let's proceed in the manner that men do in the business world today. When young men are trained for the banking business, they must become expertly familiar with a genuine dollar. Even in the touch-and-go method of handling a dollar, they must sense in a second any lack of weight; they must know every visible identification that appears on a genuine dollar. As this knowledge becomes second-nature, they only need to see or feel a counterfeit dollar to know that it does not belong in their bank. Spurious coin is neither to be accepted from, nor handed out to, a customer. The perfect knowledge of the genuine enables them to instantly discard the worthless, no matter how closely it resembles the real and no matter how attractive it appears in itself.

In a man's spiritual life, he should be so attuned to the good and the true that his inner perception would immediately reveal to him the illusion of progress. Every man is not this fortunate, but the man who has proven for himself that real progress consists solely in opening wider and wider the channels of his being, for the more complete expression of Good — when he finds himself tuning into attributes which do not belong to God — such as envy, jealousy, covetousness, selfishness, churlishness, greed, fear, worry, illness — he knows that something is amiss. He knows, also, that God, by His very nature, *can never cease giving*, so it must be that man has stopped the outflow and produced stagnation. He knows that his business is to open up the outflow, so that greater good can come in again. Sometimes if this passage has become clogged with silt, it is impossible to dynamite it and open the channel with a powerful dredge, instantly clearing the way, and it becomes necessary to remove the silt a grain at a time.

But the man who has not accepted this teaching, or who has not even been privileged to hear it, and therefore knows nothing about the ever availability of Good, thinking only in terms of the social standards around him, might he not be

fooled — easily tricked — by the illusion of progress? How is progress determined by the people
around us? Is it not gauged by our style of
living, social position and influence in the community? It is a sad commentary on the progress
of the world that this influence is determined by
our bank account, rather than our character. Of
course, influence of character will be shown, but
those who display it will not, on that account, be
listed among the successful. For admission to
the list of those who have made most progress,
the ability to make money, in the common estimate, will be the chief essential. Someone has
expressed it quite aptly: "What religion was to
the Jew, what philosophy was to the Greek, what
learning was to the Renaissance, business has
become to Europe and America. In the United
States and the British Empire, it is far beyond
all other. Success, therefore, in the minds of these
peoples, is material success, and not much more."

In the face of this, it is small wonder that we
have all had the experience of being fooled by the
illusion of progress. We have seen families that,
according to the recognized standards, were progressing — their houses were more pretentious,
their incomes larger, their cars more expensive,

119

and their prestige higher. Everybody commented: "My how that family is progressing. See how they are moving up in the world." Then suddenly we discovered that they were not progressing. The inner life of the home was not developing.

And just as many of us as individuals have had the same experience: larger salaries, more popularity, extended prestige and wider influence. We were going ahead and we thought change indicated advance. We were fooled by the external equipment of things. We were tricked by the world's standards into supposing that such things meant progress, and then suddenly we are startled by the inner voice: "What shall it profit a man if he gain the whole world and lose his own soul?" And if we get bigness and lose human values like love and friendship and confidence and integrity, where shall we be? Suddenly it is borne in upon us that there is a limit to what we can get out of *things*. We would be foolish to think we could get more than two ounces of liquid out of a 2-oz. bottle, and "we can get no more out of things than things can give, and they are not of God. The destinies of the race are within the soul."

Harry Emerson Fosdick says: "In any land, at

any time. the standards of success are a social creation. We, the people, determine what shall be called success. There have been times and places, as in the city of Florence, Italy, where to be a great person was to be a great artist, and all the people acclaimed his glory. You may be sure that if, in this country, material success has been our god, we the people have put him on his throne and kept him there. We have kowtowed and salaamed to that kind of success. We have wanted it desperately for ourselves, even when we have missed it."

If you have read thus far, I cannot believe that you would choose the *illusion of progress*, when you know there is a way by which you can recognize real progress? If you actually want to grow, from a sure footing to a larger and larger expansion of life, you will probably come to see progress, in the first place in the work itself, and only in the second place will you consider the reward. Basil King speaks of this: "Work is that contribution to the common good, which the individual has the aptitude and the ability to make. It is the highest and broadest reach of my powers of self-expression. It is the biggest outlet that I know anything about for my energies. But, most

121

of all, it is *my* contribution to the common good. It gives me the privilege of benefiting others. I am in the advantageous position of having something to bestow. Having something to bestow is always a matter of pride with us. What we give should please those to whom it is offered and do credit to ourselves. In working for others, I also have the consciousness that others are working for me! All the world is mine, with all doing things for my benefit. In the community in which I live, every individual may be considered as in active service for my good. Success is *the full expansion of myself for the common good.*"

This idea of success, or progress, by contribution, rather than by acquisition, is what Ernest Holmes teaches us in his article on "The Law of Circulation," in which he says in part: "Because of the unity underlying all life, no man lives entirely unto himself, but through himself he lives unto the whole, *which whole embodies all other lives.* Therefore, 'he that findeth his life, shall lose it; and he that loseth his life, for My sake, shall find it'. When a man's thoughts rest entirely upon himself, he becomes abnormal and unhappy; but when he gives himself with enthusiasm to any legitimate purpose, losing himself in the thing which he is doing, he becomes normal and happy. (Only as much life enters into us as we can conceive, and we conceive of life in the largest sense only when there is complete abandonment to it.) The losing of personality in the great sea of life which surrounds us, makes possible the flow of this life through our own livingness, producing the inevitable reaction of a greater livingness in our own lives."

Does this not begin to give us a different conception of progress?

In the renewed building activity over the entire country, and the attendant obstructions spread in every direction—lumber, cement, carts, bricks, boardings, and even in the perennial reconstruction of the roadways themselves — a metaphysician was led to remark that it would almost appear to be inevitable that "where humanity endeavors to construct, there obstruction arises, like a stumbling-block, to irritate, confuse, and delay." Those of us who have been fooled by the illusion of progress can understand this; as even those of us who have held steadfastly to what we have recognized as *real* progress have, at times, felt a sense of adverse forces swinging against us, causing discord, inharmony and lack. We know, however, that anything that appears to be a stumbling-block, an obstruction, to our progress is merely a false belief in separation from God. By spiritual understanding, we learn that this seeming block to our progress only occurs when we forget our Oneness with Good; only when we forget our privilege and power to reflect all the beautiful, useful and joyous ideas resident in divine Mind. As we think in this manner, we are engaging in true constructive work — real progress — and to the appearing of these spiritual verities, evil can oppose no stumbling-block.

Out of the experience today, we will know a greater good tomorrow, so there will always be expansion. When we speak of this oneness, this unity of God and man, we are not referring to uniformity. It is not something produced by levelling either up or down. No true vision of life offers such a view as that. On the contrary, we agree with Emerson that: "Every man who is worthy the name is a non-conformist." So we are not suggesting as a plan for progress a unity that means oneness in the individual gifts of ability. But, in spite of all our differences, "some kind of unity does lie at the basis of the life of humanity, and binds all into one great whole;

yet such a unity can be found only in the inner life of man."

Fichte, the great German philosopher, says: "An insight into the absolute unity of the human existence with the divine is certainly the profoundest knowledge that man can attain. When he realizes that the divine life and energy actually live in him; then, whatever comes to pass around him, nothing will appear strange or unaccountable. He knows that he is in God's world and that nothing can be done that does not directly tend to good. His whole outward existence flows forth softly and gently, from his inner being, and issues out into reality without difficulty or hindrance."

That, to me, is genuine progress. I don't think we could find a finer description of that perfect union with Universal Life; that conscious recognition that individually we are God expressing as us at the point of our comprehension, which eventuates in a certainty that every move we make is a step in real progress. This unity must have been an actual experience in the consciousness of Buddha, Socrates, Plotinus, Paul, St. Francis of Assissi, Tolstoi, Emerson, Whitman, Lincoln, and, above all, Jesus Christ, whose consciousness was clearer and more profound than any other. This unity comes from the conscious recognition that God is All-in-all, the Source of all our being. Whether we call this Source, First Cause, Creator, Life, Love, Truth, Mind or God, the fact remains that the same infinite energy has found expression through all.

And the men of the past who have entered most profoundly into this consciousness of unity with God and man have been thoroughly convinced of their unity with the universe, as well. It was centuries ago that the Greek philosopher, Pythagoras, uttered the great truth that "Man is a microcosm of God," meaning that the universe on a large scale is what man is on a small. It is claimed that no one has ever declared his conscious unity with God without at the same time experiencing a oneness with the universe. As John Herman Randall, in "The Spirit of the New Philosophy" said:

"If the unity we are striving to attain in human life is to be worth all the prodigious sacrifices men have made, then it must possess such a profound moral and spiritual content as shall give birth to a new Spirit in man, re-vitalizing, all-compelling, and universal."

126

(This does not mean that we are attempting to unify with people, but with the Principle of Life behind all people and things.) This is working from the center rather than the circumference, for in the One Mind are the minds of all people. I do not wish any of this to sound abstract or abstruse, but it seems wiser to me to give you one principle, the application of which will insure you that all your steps will be upward, rather than to attempt specific instructions for the solution of each individual problem. The latter course would be certain to omit the very one that would be most important to you. (As it is, if you can begin each day with a conscious realization of your oneness with all Good, then all your day's duties will automatically be progressive.) "Thus will God, the whole, find Himself in man, the part, as man becomes conscious of his true being; and thus will man, the part, find himself in God and of God, the whole" and it will further be said: "At last, God knows Himself as God in man. At last, man knows himself as man in God."

(The mind naturally demands of itself that there shall be a Presence and a Power in the universe, which shall sustain it, and without this

knowledge or conviction, one cannot even ana-
lyze progress.) God does not think of anyone as
standing still or lost, but such a man is lost to
himself, to his greater possibility, to his higher
hope — to the deeper meaning of life, until he
locates this Power or Presence.   We need to
resurrect our ideas of reality. (Every man needs
to awaken the God that is within him, and then
the God within him shall go forth into creation.)
We are like dead people, so far as using our full
power is concerned, but the Spirit within us never
died and never will; and that is why, no matter
where man's intellect may have taken him—into
confusion, into grief, into despair and fear—there
is always an inner voice saying:("Christ in me is
life, and the life in me is the light and the life
of God.")

If you are working for the right kind of progress, it will include money, when you need money,
but you will not be burdened with money when
you do not need it. (Having given your attention
to Mind, you will not have to give your attention
to *things*.) You will be able to wield the power
which produces and controls things. You will be
amazed at your accomplishments when you try.
You need give no concern to the rich returns

128

that will come to you, if you will use your rich ideas.

The one great principle governing your life and mine, whether we are aware of it or not, is: "Give and it shall be given unto you; good measure, pressed down, shaken together, running over." This, however, does not mean that we are to divide our time, half of our time to giving and half to receiving. If we are trying to get warm, we do not give half our time to heat and half to cold. We work with the principle of heat and leave the other part of the problem to take care of itself. So it is with giving. (We concern ourselves wholly with the giving, and the receiving end takes care of itself.) If you seem to be experiencing great lack — no matter how it is manifested, lack of health, lack of friends, lack of money — so that you are certain you have nothing with which to give, then *you, above all people, must begin giving at once* To delay doing so would be like a very sick woman, under a doctor's care, stating she would follow his directions for health when she got well when to all intents and purposes her life depended upon her following his instructions *in order to get well.*

Perhaps the very finest thing you could give

would be an idea. And you have no good ideas?
If you have an ideal — and who hasn't an ideal?
— you have an idea. The way in which you can
express this ideal will be revealed to you alone.
(When next you feel this inner urge, pushing out
into life, heed it.) When you have thus learned
to work with the giving end, knowing that good
results must follow, life will become a thrilling
adventure. You will be astounded at how much
better the things are which you attract now than
before you were aware of this Principle underlying your life. When you feel tempted to force
your good, as most of us do at times, because
you think it is not coming as rapidly as you
would like, just think how much finer it is going
to be when you allow it to come of its own accord.

On this matter of giving, I would like to remind you, when you are saying you have nothing
you can give, (anything that is *saved* is likely to
get rusty — *even ideas.*) (When an idea comes to
you, *that is the time when it carries its strongest
propulsion,* so put it to work at once.) If you
keep it, you are postponing your greater good,
for back of the first idea are many more *prosper-
ing* ideas, and *they cannot come forth until the
release of your first idea releases them* Isn't that

a thought to galvanize us into action? Someone has further elucidated it thus:

"In any realm, if one abstracts an idea from its appropriate task, and tries to keep it in isolation as a mere belief, it always dries up. The only way we can keep an idea (any kind of an idea) real and vital is to do something with it. A generation ago, a prominent professor in Yale University, described the process by which he lost many of his religious beliefs: 'It was as if I had put my beliefs into a drawer, and when I opened it, there was nothing there at all'. Inevitably so! Take one look at the life of Jesus and be convinced that the last place where it would be possible to keep any little faith surrounding Him, would be in a drawer."

Yet, we find ourselves doing something similar to that, do we not? We have a number of lovely ideas about God and man, which we put away in a drawer, expecting to use them. When sorrow strikes us deeply, we remember that we have comforting ideas — consoling ideas — which we stored away, and when we hunt them up, we find them so withered, there is no warmth or aroma in them!

We know that deeds are far more convincing

than arguments, and we know that the most convincing persuasiveness in life lies in right deeds.
Our whole purpose is to stimulate you to such
deeds. We know that Christian living can be
done. And the man who has entered into a state
of wholeness and completion no longer walks the
earth as downtrodden, disconsolate and afraid.
He knows this: that Heaven is here, and that
God is his Host. And he has further learned the
great lesson which all people must learn: that we
are today potentially that perfect, divine being.
We do not have to acquire divinity; we merely
have to reveal that divinity which ever indwells.
In this, there can be no illusion of progress!

CHAPTER VII

"If Prayers Are Answered, Why Not Mine?"

THERE is still confusion in the minds of people on this subject of prayer, as evidenced by the question heading this chapter. Another comment that is made when people would push their good from them is: "My mother has prayed for me and my minister has prayed that I might find a position, and they are two of the best people on earth. If their prayers were not answered, why would God hear anyone?" All of these queries indicate the false assumption that prayers are answered in proportion to the "goodness" of the one praying. This is true only when by *goodness* we mean one of clear perception . . . one who never loses sight of the allness of Good and man's unity with It.

If we can better understand the nature of the God to whom we pray; the extent of His power, His attitude toward our requests, and the requisite for successful petition, it is likely we shall better comprehend why such questions are asked. These may seem unimportant points, but they are not nearly as foolish as the manner in which we approach God. The superficial evidence, as gathered from the testimony of thousands of different individuals, is to the effect that God answers *some* prayers, but not every prayer! If this be true, there must be a reason back of it.

It is hardly likely that anyone reading these words is still thinking of God as in the nature of a magnified human being, occupying a throne in the sky, bestowing favors on a certain few, and punishing others for doing things which He is supposed to have made them capable of doing. Surely it is not possible for the average intelligent individual to conceive of God as being able to eternally torture any of His offspring; or that an infinitely good God could send sickness or destruction upon His children. We prefer to accept the God of the Scriptures, as the One and only Creator; with a creation that is spiritual and good. Spirit, God, is necessarily omnipotent, omniscient, and omnipresent.

If, however, you have prayed to a God, whom you were not quite certain of contacting; if you have thought that His hand was only showering blessings upon you *when* you prayed to Him, then we can understand why your prayers were not answered. You were not recognizing Omnipotence! God cannot change His nature. He is forever giving, impartially, to "the just and the unjust alike." Therefore, one of the things we need to know — whether we are suffering from a thought of disease (lack of health) or lack of money, or lack of friends — is that our Father was not a party to our "undoing."

Regardless of what you tell us, we take the startling position that *all prayer is answered!* Our reason for this is that the Creator, and everything created, is governed and maintained by law. So, when, in an effort to explain why prayers are not answered, St. John says:("They ask and receive not, because they ask amiss," this simply conveys to us that somewhere along the line there has not been a <u>compliance with the law governing prayer.)</u> If that is so, then it is not true prayer, for all real prayer would have to be uttered in line with the law of its life. Hence our statement that *all true prayer is answered.*

The author is most eager to impart to you such information as she has on this subject of

135

prayer, in the hope that you may never again feel, in any sense, that you are removed from all the Power there is in the universe, for the truth is, you have only to turn to the God within, and you have *immediate* access to all Good. The only reason that sometimes individual prayers appear to go unanswered, and those of teacher or minis- ter seem to be heard, is that religious teachers and practitioners are more familiar with the law regarding prayer; they have made such knowl- edge an integral part of their being. The law itself has to be impartial and would work for the prisoner in San Quentin just as quickly as for you and me, if he understood its principle and application.

There is no one who will dispute my statement when I say that darkness is merely the absence of light, yet there are those who are ready to take issue when I say that sin is ignorance — a mis- take, and needs only to be corrected, in line with the laws which govern — yet, most of you realize that all unhappiness springs from a disturbed mental condition. We must correct and disci- pline our thinking, if we would eliminate the sin of ignorance, and its consequent results. Disci- pline and routine are monotonous and our first impulse is to flee from them. Have you ever thought how athletes willingly go through their training of weeks, months, maybe years? They know they cannot successfully compete if they have not disciplined themselves through proper training.

Yet, we hope to realize for ourselves and others the greatest power in the universe—the Presence of God — by thinking about it perhaps a few minutes each day. (When we pray, or meditate, we release a thought, an animating, pulsating *conviction*.) We know that our word is power; that it gives form to our desires, and we release it into subjective mind, with the knowledge that it cannot return unto us void. But this is not done by a half hour's contemplation on Sunday morning. (Our power must come from constant communion with God.) As Ghandi answered a Swiss General, who inquired of him what, in his opinion, were the necessary qualities of a great leader, and Ghandi's instant response was, "A man in constant touch with God." (The avenues of our mind must be kept open to the inflow of Truth; we must *abide* in the consciousness of perfection, if we expect by our prayers to lift either ourselves or others into a state of harmony.)

137

As we resolve the entire problem of prayer into a mental proposition, we find it easier. We think of God as one Mind, everywhere present. If God is Mind, then all the intelligence we have comes from It. If we desire more knowledge and wisdom, we need only establish a closer contact with this Mind. We came forth from God, out of this One Mind, and we continue to exist in It. As we understand the real character of God, we no longer pray to some far off Being. We know that we need only to get still and turn our attention within. As we abide in "the secret place of the Most High," within us, we are conscious of our union with the One Being, and we dwell on the love of God, until the peace and harmony of divine love fill our soul with gladness. The subjective mind will then receive only thoughts of love, and Love is the most potent factor in the universe.

Someone has described earnest desire as prayer; certainly not a mere wishy-washy desire could be called prayer, but the deep longing of our nature must be prayer. In the book of Revelation, there is a lovely line: "Behold I stand at the door and knock. If any man hear my voice and open the door, I will come in to him and sup with him

and he with me." A beautiful picture of in-
timacy, like the interchange of reciprocal senti-
ment, as it were . . . A vivid description of
prayer, which need not necessarily be either petition or even thanksgiving. "It is the flinging
open the door that the Supreme Guest may come
in," as King says.

By the words, "asking amiss," we are not to
suppose that the trouble is that there are some
things God would not want to give us; the attitude is all wrong that supposes there are certain
blessings that God withholds but possibly if He
is cajoled sufficiently — perhaps if He is told a
little more in detail the urgency of our need —He
will be persuaded to change His mind and grant
our request. This is truly "asking amiss." God
is not only governed by law, He is Law, the
Principle back of everything, as the Bible says:
"For I, Jehovah, change not."

If you have been praying for supply — abundance — and you seem to have less and less, do
not say "I guess God thinks it is not best for me
to have it." (Jesus said that he came that we
might have life more abundantly.) Men do not
need to be poor to be righteous. But, there is
a law governing this, as all other relations of life.

139

There is a righteous law of accumulation. This law is "Seek ye first the kingdom of God and His righteousness; and all these things shall be added unto you." (We are not denied houses or lots or automobiles, stocks, bonds, or stables, but all of these things are "added.") If it does not suit us to follow the _law_ of acquisition, we shall always find it a hit or miss game. What would happen in our daily relations with our fellow men if we suddenly decided to change the standards, the laws, by which business had been transacted? Suppose we decide that 5¢ should be enough postage for a Special Delivery letter, have we the slightest assurance that it would be delivered other than regular mail? Suppose I have been giving 16 oz. to the pound on certain articles in my grocery store and I suddenly decide that 9 oz. should be a pound, would I not soon lose my customers because of my dishonesty?

It seems to me, the only assurance we have that this law of accumulation will be continually operative in our lives is for us to keep both the letter and the spirit of it. We can now understand the text: "He that seeth with a bountiful eye will be blessed." It is based on exact law. (Jesus demonstrated that abundance is to be found

in the kingdom of God, and *when that kingdom
is found,* everything needful will be found.)

Have you ever thought of the fact that there
is a type of praying that does harm? that makes
the condition worse than it was when we began
to pray? Many times, when the need seems greatest, we magnify the condition we would be rid of,
rather than that for which we pray. We tell God
how terribly sick we are, or our wife is, or someone else who is dear to us and who is the object
of our prayer . . . and then we plead with Him
to change the condition. What is uppermost in
our mind is our *need,* and one requires only a
fundamental knowledge of psychology to realize
that as we pray in that fashion, we become
"sicker." (The subjective mind takes our strongest thought, our deep conviction — which in this
case is that we are terribly sick — and brings it
back to us, SICK. We must know the law so
thoroughly that all that is necessary is for us to
affirm the presence of Good: "The Lord *is* my
shepherd. I *shall not* want. He *maketh* me to lie
down in green pastures. He *leadeth* me beside
the still waters. He *restoreth* my soul." The
affirmation lifts our thought above the pain which
is disturbing us.

(Actually, prayer is the art and the science of inducing, within consciousness, concepts of definite desires, *as already accomplished facts and experiences in life!*) For does not the promise read: "Before they call, will I answer," a truth which we must perfectly understand, if we know the law of prayer. This matter of giving thanks for a blessing which we have not yet received in the objective world, is one of humanity's worst stumbling-blocks. A friend recently gave me a helpful thought on this. She often shops in a distant city, and her orders are sent to a friend who makes the purchase. When her order is sent, she thanks her friend "in advance for her kindness." She accepts it as being already purchased the minute her letter is mailed, and she gives it no further thought except to prepare for the reception and use of the article she has ordered. Isn't that a helpful thought? All of us have done that so many times. Certainly, then, we can depend on the promises of God to an even greater degree than we could ever depend on the word of any earthly friend. His promise is that, in the case of our prayer, *it is answered before the request even goes forth!*

Real prayer embraces that faith which is referred to as "the substance of things hoped for, the evidence of things not seen." We realize, then, to be true, effective, and in accordance with divine Principle, we must have the faith that Jesus had, when he raised Lazarus . . . "Father, I thank thee that thou hast heard me, and I thank thee that thou hearest me always." It is no violation of logic to claim our desires as already having been met, and the reasonableness and truth of such a claim are unavoidable conclusions, in view of the Unity of Being and man's at-one-ment with It. Our wishes are already gratified, if they be consistent with Reality; our questions are already answered and the answer is always the thing itself, but it does require our recognition and acceptance to perceive objectively the present possession of that for which we are praying.

In the face of all appearance to the contrary, we must hold steadfast to the truth that God is Good and that good is all. And furthermore that Good is all-powerful. No matter if we are surrounded by the lame, the halt, and the blind, we must still know that God is Good and that Good is the One and only power.

Do you recall that Shelley attributed his mo-

143

ments of genius to a Power, greater than himself, yet always at hand, as answer to the prayer of utter sincerity? As we approach, in a measure the life of supreme good, we glimpse the glory of spiritual progress. This purified consciousness is "a transparency, through which the healing light of Truth and Love blesses and heals."

God can only contemplate Himself as Being, certainly never as desiring or having or acquiring. (*Having* would imply ownership outside the self, so God, the Universal Self, cannot possess: He must always *be*, for nothing exists outside of Him.) Since we are made in the image and likeness of God, we must reproduce the divine nature. We can have no quality underived from God and we must be all that the divine nature is! Therefore, man is, and has, all that the universe is, *within himself*. Regardless of how the outer man claims to own things, *no one actually possesses.* (No one can know or experience anything outside of himself.)

Perhaps you will ask, if the good which we desire, and pray for, is not objectified, where are we to conceive of this good now as present? WITHIN OURSELVES. (It is within us that we shall find all that we need) with which to express

144

life. As God creates His universe, by knowing Himself to be It, so we must sense within our own minds that we are the objects of our desires, and that they are complete and perfect experiences right this moment. Only by being filled to overflowing with Spirit, shall we know abundance; only by becoming Love and Harmony shall we know Love and Harmony. God never changes, but growth and unfoldment take place in our lives, as we realize our oneness with the Principle that governs the Universe, and gain an understanding of the Law, which — when used constructively—frees us from sickness, lack and limitation.

Real man, made in the image and likeness of God, is free, and in proportion as we understand this, we have power over every limited thought. All prayer is answered on the principle that subjective mind externalizes on the body, and the body of our affairs, whatever is impressed upon it by conscious mind. So, if we wish perfect freedom, the belief in ourselves as *pure spirit* — not subject to sickness, limitation, or lack — must be impressed upon subjective mind.

If you are unable to think in terms of "conscious mind" and "subjective mind," which is merely by way of differentiating the work of the One Mind,— perhaps you would like only to use the term "God" in your praying; then you have only to get still and know that Spirit is the fulfillment of all your desires. This recognition has the power to bring the invisible forth into form as you desire. Remember "Thou shalt also decree a thing, and it shall be established unto thee."

Begin first with the knowledge that God is life, truth, love, intelligence, omnipotence, omniscience, omnipresence. As you cling to this steadfast belief in God as the only Power, you will see all seeming evil and discord melt away.

Then, remember that every moment of your life you are a child of God, and that His wisdom, His Power, His love, are flowing through you; His strength is your strength; His perfection is your perfection; His abundance is your complete supply. If you can fill your consciousness with all that *is*, you will not need to deny anything.

If you are willing that God's will shall manifest in your life — and this will is always for your good — you will not need to ask for each specific thing you want. When you are really desiring the kingdom of God, all supply will come forth spontaneously. Then, never again will you say your prayer is not answered. The very Spirit of truth is at your call, and will "guide you into all truth about all things."

CHAPTER VIII

The Dry-rot of Self-deception

ON MY WAY home one night recently, I found the street passage completely blocked by moving vans . . . five, six, perhaps ten . . . all in front of an imposing looking apartment house. Every tenant in it was moving out simultaneously! The incident was so unusual, except in case of fire or earthquake, that I inquired the cause, only to be told that the owner of the building had, the night before, discovered that his building was literally ruined by dry-rot!

The outside remained beautiful and majestic looking, built to endure the disintegrating effects of weather without an impress; the inside, to all appearances, modern to the moment . . . the last word in elegance, comfort, and artistic surroundings. And now it was problematical whether any portion of the building could be saved, either by expense or ingenuity. Yet, what an easy matter it would have been had this dry-rot been discovered in its incipiency, and that portion of the diseased sill (or fire wall) been removed!

The incident set me to thinking . . . about myself, about you. I wondered how many of us are walking around with our friends, satisfied with the results we are getting from life — maybe receiving much love and admiration — when all the while our character, our chances of any heaven here and hereafter, are being slowly, but insidiously, destroyed by the dry-rot of self-deception. Can it be possible, do you suppose?

Prior to the last century, it was the common indulgence to attempt to deceive *other people* about ourselves. If we found ourselves filled with inhibitions, terrible inferiority complexes, we immediately assumed a superiority complex, believing we were leaving an impression of importance on our fellow-men. No longer can we imagine this. With the general dissemination of psychological information, even the masses now recognize this as only a defense mechanism. And, since Emerson uttered his now famous remark: "What you are speaks so loud I cannot hear what you say," we reluctantly face the fact that we don't get very far in fooling *others*. But what about ourselves? If we think we are build-

THE DRY-ROT OF SELF-DECEPTION

ing and maintaining, in this "temple of the Holy Ghost," something enduring and beautiful; and when we come to take stock of ourselves, if we discover that only in outward appearance is this true, then we have certainly been betrayed by *the dry-rot of self-deception.* With the remotest possibility of such an outcome, it behooves us to take stock now.

How would this likely come about? It would all have to be in our mental attitude toward life, wouldn't it? Then it might be well to consider whether or not we have a capacity for elevated vision. What is our conception of friendship, ambition, joy, influence, possessions? Our attitude toward one or all of these will be enlightening. Numerous people have claimed that you can determine what a man is by knowing his friends; others have said his ambitions give him away, while others still contend that to know a man we need to determine the influence he exerts in the circle in which he moves.

Tennyson said "Worse than being fooled by others is to fool oneself," so he recognized the existence of self-deception. In no other one thing perhaps do we fool ourselves more than in our attitude toward "possessions." It is one of the all-absorbing endeavors of a life time . . . this acquiring possessions. "My own." How much charm we find in those words, and how long it takes us to find out their worth. How we cling to things! And, it seems, the longer we live, the closer we come to that place where we can carry none of them, the more tenaciously we cling to them! Increasing our possessions is actually increasing our troubles, unless we know, with all our being, that "the one single use of things, which we call our own, is that they may be his who hath need of them." Unless we have come to this knowledge, we are greatly deceiving ourselves with regard to our possessions. We have repeatedly stated, in this book, and in our classes, that you can have what you wish, but you must take what goes with it. We have assured you that it is the Father's good will for us to have abundance — for us to enjoy all that will make us comfortable and contribute to our growth and usefulness — but, it is now necessary for us to add a final word to this: *no possessions are good, but by the good use we make of them!* With this in mind, let's refrain from what Bailey calls "the first and worst of all frauds — cheating one's self."

Strange as this may sound to you, we can do ourselves untold harm in our attitude toward ourselves. No, I do not mean the "sin" of egotism or egoism, but rather that of depreciation. Or course I am not speaking of that mock modesty which makes us try to fool another by depreciating our own accomplishments. I am speaking of the manner in which we deceive ourselves when we are continually unmindful, and unappreciative, of our present blessings. It is a habit with women to look at someone whom they think "altogether lovely," and immediately depreciate their own appearance. They wish their eyes were larger, their feet smaller, their hair more lustrous, their skin of finer texture. What are we doing as we have such thoughts? We are "cursing" the good looks we have. We are giving to subjective mind a *strong* thought of our poor equipment, and this picture will be perpetuated. Subjective mind will have to create eyes not as good, hands not as beautiful, bodies not as agile, and skin of coarser texture, and so on, for we are giving it a poor pattern. If, in doing this, we are expecting to become more and more beautiful, we are deceiving ourselves. My friends, this is not the manner by which we increase our charms.

153

We do not study *imperfection* and hope thereby to become more perfect. We are deceiving ourselves when we fail to praise the God within for every "good and perfect gift." In praising the self, we are not becoming conceited because of some personal qualification or aptness; we are thanking God that every man is made "in His image and likeness," and is therefore innately perfect — able to bring forth into expression that which is like its Creator — wholly Good.

How completely we deceive ourselves about what we are accomplishing, was vividly brought home to me in a young woman who meant to become "important" and produced death. The girl at twenty found herself slightly behind in her studies, and, because of an invalid mother, it began to look as if she might not have an even chance in acquiring "fame and fortune," Not being able to endure the thought of being inconspicuous, she decided her best opportunity was to make herself a permanent invalid, thus becoming the center of attention.

At first, she complained of her heart, but the physician assured the family there was neither organic nor functional heart trouble, but she held steadfastly to her statement and remained in bed. Subsequently, she announced that the heart had produced dropsy. The doctor pointed out that she was painfully thin and no indentation of the flesh even suggested dropsy, but she *would* have it, and she eventually did—both the heart trouble and the dropsy.

But subjective mind had no way of knowing anything but what she insisted upon . . . that she had heart trouble and dropsy . . . so it could only create that for her. She produced in her experience that which she relentlessly maintained. And the beautiful young woman deceived herself, alone, of all the world. She hadn't an idea of dying; she expected to live to a ripe old age, having people look after her and administer to her wants . . . always the center of attention. Some men describe this as the "will to power." Freud calls it "the desire to be great," while John Dewey speaks of it as "the desire to be important."

We are not discussing today those people whom are classified as having definite "mental kinks," but we are talking of the individual, like you and I, who thinks he is doing pretty well for himself, and all the while may be completely destroyed by the dry-rot of self-deception.

If we call ourselves acquiring intelligence and with it fail to get understanding, we are greatly deceiving ourselves. David Seabury calls our attention to the fact that, undoubtedly, Leopold and Loeb, whose lives were so publicised, possessed unusually high intelligent quotients, and "might easily have exceeded either Emerson or Lincoln in straight brain power," but in our wildest imagination, we could not think of them as having understanding. This brings forcibly to our minds how the acquisition of knowledge, without understanding, is one thing in which we deceive ourselves greatly.

Another pathetic situation that sometimes arises in our lives is when things do not go our way, when affliction strikes us or disaster overtakes us, and we allow our sweetness to turn to wormwood and gall. We think we are "paying the world back," by paying it in its own coin. We harden our hearts and — embittered, sarcastic and cynical — we meet the days. We fool ourselves again. We are not hurting the world; it is fool proof, but we are hurting ourselves. We are daily creating for ourselves a new crop of the very things we so despise, think so much about, and tie to us with cords of many fibers. God did not send upon us any disaster, any hardship, any affliction. *His will is always good.* But, at least, we should be able to say as did Longfellow "It has done me good to be somewhat parched by the heat and drenched by the rain of life," when sorrows and disappointments *do* overtake us. It is foolish to hang on to the dross, when we find we are already in the fiery furnace. Just there is the place to drop it and our composition will necessarily be purer afterwards. A good fire is guaranteed to liquefy the gold and harden the clay. A generous vine, if never pruned, runs all to stems, and finally becomes weak and fruitless. So, even though we may resent our desires being checked, we later find strength and growth filling our being; and we must not fool ourselves and think we have chosen the better way when we allow ourselves to become embittered.

I find I haven't space to talk on friendship, as I had planned, except to remind you that we are on the wrong track "when we think of friendship as something to *get*, rather than something to give." Less has been written about *enemies*, and I want to stress that a bit now. Benjamin Franklin believed that there are no *little* enemies. He believed that the most insignificant enemy was likely to do one harm, and he went to great length to convert enemies into friends . . . even to the extent of *asking a favor of the enemy!* This was not bad psychology. It calls to mind the story about King Ptolemy, who was reproached by his associates for rewarding, instead of destroying, his enemies. "What," said the man of great understanding, "do I not destroy my enemies, when I make them my friends?" Our enemies must be transmuted into friends by the alchemy of love. One never becomes rich enough that he can safely indulge himself in the pleasure of having even one enemy.

The only way we can be certain that we shall not suffer from his hands is to follow the example of King Ptolmey and make him our friend. The worst enemies we have are not those to whom we have done a wrong but those who know they have done us an evil. They cannot forgive us that we have provoked them to the point that they have become our enemy. Destroy such a man with kindness, so that what he is, ceases to be. How can we avoid indulging in enemies, you ask? Bishop Hall once said: "There is no enemy can hurt us but our own hands. Satan could not hurt us, if our own corruption betrayed us not.

Afflictions cannot hurt us without our own impatience. Temptations cannot hurt us without our yielding." If we insist on loving an enemy, in our mind he exists only as a friend, no matter what his attitude toward us. And *in our mind is the only place that any person ever touches our world;* our business, then, is only to love our enemy! As Dr. Fosdick says: "Hating people is like burning down your home to get rid of a rat."

A young matron said to me last week, "My position is becoming intolerable. I must maintain my own self-respect. I cannot longer remain silent. I must tell him what I think of him!" Solomon's aphorism, as you recall, was "He that is slow to anger is better than the mighty; and he that ruleth his spirit than he that taketh a city." It must be plain to all of us that no one can ever become great who is unable to control his emotion. Napoleon's oft-repeated remark was that he could control men, as long as he could keep his anger below his chin. We are all familiar with the devastating physical results of not controlling our emotions. Anger is like poison poured into the blood; in fact, many labeled poisons are far less harmful. And worry, verily, leaves a calcareous deposit around the joints, which result in rheumatism and arthritis. These are the results of repeated tests made by reputable research men. How silly we are to see no further than our noses! I told the young woman she *could* certainly tell her husband what she thought of him, if she were compelled to have momentary emotional relief. I told her she could change the annoyance of the moment into permanent physical suffering — real agony — if she chose, as is often done. "Right now," I added, "there is harmony between you two, and harmony is a constructive force which builds, and will eventually lift you out of the spot you are now in, where you are feeling a little pressure for fear he will think you are losing your spirit, merely because you allow him the freedom of speaking and acting as he likes. Yes, you can give him 'a piece of your mind' but you will as surely be deceiving yourself as to the final outcome . . . about what really brings lasting happiness . . . as if you made up your mind to prepare forever to live in the dark! When we come right down to it, the only conquest we are ever called upon to make is the conquest over self . . . just one conquest, but it may mean many battles."

Most of us certainly have in mind the purpose

to make our influence on the side of right. Of course, we consciously try to influence each other. Particularly do we do this with members of our family or with close friends, but even here, the *unconscious* influence would sometimes startle us. We need to be reminded of this occasionally, lest we drop into the habit of thinking our influence stops just where we have planned.

There is what we term a conscious, conventional influence, like attending Church on Sunday morning; like belonging to the best literary club in our town; like contributing as generously as possible to worthy enterprises; like purchasing our home in the best locality. When we have attended to these and many things like them, we are apt to think everyone must know about our splendid influence. It is not at all impossible that our unconscious influence may counteract every bit of this! It doesn't require a prodigy of enlightenment to recognize that we may fool ourselves terribly in the matter of our influence. Naturally, if we are blessed with a sincere desire to bring out in every person an expression of the omnipresence of God, then our unconscious influence will necessarily add weight to our conscious influence.

161

Someone has said that to realize how little any of us are missed in the world, how much we are really needed, one need only put his finger in a bucket of water and then remove it and see how much impression remains. This remark is both true and false. True, if we think of the importance of one individual as compared to all the millions on earth; false, if we would even suggest that a single individual has no influence. We are connected with our fellowmen by a thousand fibers and along these sympathetic threads "our actions run as causes and come back to us as effects." And Thomas à Kempis believed that no influence ever dies; that every act, emotion, look or word carries an influence for good or evil, through all eternity. As some one has said: "There is no action of man in this life which is not the beginning of so long a chain of consequences, as no human providence can tell what the end will be."

But what about the *unconscious* influence I am leaving on the hearts and minds of my associates? What of my chauffeur who daily observes my lavish expenditures but is never able to persuade me to give him a raise? What of my hair-dresser, to whom I have handed our literature, but when the time comes for my tip, it takes me five minutes to get my folded currency out of the way so I can locate a couple of nickles for her. What does she think of my generosity? Does she want to know more of the Truth which will enable us to recognize the abundance of supply as ever-present, *as evidenced by my giving*, or does she think the understanding she now has is a better one? What about the telephone girl (just recovering from an illness) who nervously gives me the wrong number, and I rebuke her in no uncertain terms, and threaten to report her to the supervisor? What does that little girl think about my Christlike spirit? Does she think it is "more to be desired than rubies?" I think not. What about the man in the gas station who, in order to establish a little more friendly relationship, talks to me while he services my car, and I snap him up with a quick retort, asking him what he thinks I do with my time. Am I to wait all day for such service? Can you imagine what my influence on him is? No matter who tells him I am a lovely Christian woman, he will think to himself, "Yes, I know her. I know just how much love she has in her heart."

Quarles reminds us: "The height of all philosophy is to know thyself; and the end of this knowledge is to know God. Know thyself that thou mayest know God; and know God that thou mayest love Him and be like Him. In the one thou art *initiated* into wisdom; and in the other *perfected* in it." If you are recognizing and maintaining your spiritual identity, then you are one with God. If you are doing *any less than this, you are fooling yourself when you think your influence is for the greatest good.* Only when your conscious influence is such that every man who comes into your presence feels that he has seen something of God, can you feel satisfied with your influence. Recognizing yourself as a spiritual being, if God can sin, then you can sin. Not otherwise. Everything that touches your life is a mental fingerprint by which you are readily recognized. Let him who will limit his soul; let him who will be indifferent to his influence. For you, there is the presence of God in challenge to your capacity to receive. Let God flow through you, and life in you will become alive, beautiful, productive, and you will no longer deceive yourself about anything!

CHAPTER IX

Do We Control Our Destiny?

THERE are many great thinkers who have believed that we have little or nothing to do with controlling our destiny. Seneca believed that our fate is decreed, and that nothing comes to pass outside of what God appoints — every portion of man's sorrow and joy, therefore, being predetermined. And Goethe admitted his belief that "existence is irretrieveably under the control of destiny." On the other hand, there are men like Balfour, who have felt that "destiny" is the phrase of a weak heart, and the scapegoat behind which we hide when ashamed of our follies.

Personally, we agree with Tryon Edwards that "Thoughts lead on to purposes; purposes go forth into action; actions into habits, habits decide character; and character fixes our destiny." Just a logical manner of showing how, step by step, we control our destiny. Destiny is generally understood to convey the meaning of something foreordained, though it is used synonomously with lot, fortune, doom, and fate. As we speak of it in this article, we mean it to represent any present or future condition.

Longfellow used the expression "as inevitable as destiny," but in the face of this and similar ideas, we hope to prove to you that we assuredly do control our destiny. We control all the conditions that come within our individual worlds. As we recognize the divine creative urge within us, pushing out into expression, we know that we do not need to *react*, like a ball thrown against a wall, which must return in a predetermined manner. We know that it is our privilege to *respond* to life, and that takes cognizance of our spiritual contribution. It is then that we can lift our heads in the realization that it is we, alone, who determine our destiny; that we, alone, make life worth living, by our interior creative, spiritual contribution. An eminent divine* said in a recent sermon: "What happens to us from without does not determine the consequence. What happens to us from without pulls our triggers and explodes us. The consequence depends on what was in us to explode." It is a habit of the race,

*Rev. Harry Emerson Fosdick.

however, when we are experiencing periods of happiness and prosperity, to feel that *we* did it; when the tide turns, when the world knows we are not so prosperous, we comment on how life has treated us, what fate has decreed for us and so on.

The history of America is the history of "impossible" achievements, so there can remain little doubt than man can do practically anything he wants to do, in the way of attaining position, wealth and fame. This brief article will not stress that so much; it is too generally accepted that man makes his own place in the world of affairs today; and we have already spoken in this book of many things which will assist man in any honest undertaking. As we talk about destiny, we shall hope to leave the impression of something even more important than wealth and prestige, though these may be included. All of the good of the universe is ours as we can accept it.

What we really need, at the outset, is to find the joy of living, for until we have found the joy of living, we have not established harmonious relationship with God, whose good pleasure it is to give us the kingdom. When once we have the kingdom, it matters not where we are, for the joy of freedom, and of dominion of Spirit . . .

the authority of our divine heritage . . . makes heaven wherever we are. We should refuse to accept, from the subjectivity of any relative, ideas and opinions which are not conducive to complete expression of our divinity. We should sincerely declare that our inheritance is not from man, but from God, the Essence of Perfection.

We must learn the highest source of our ideas, for no thought can carry us beyond the plane upon which it originates. And "only from the Mind of God can come ideas that have power to lift man to the plane of his own inherent divinity." Only through the unfoldment and understanding of our highest ideas, which relate us to the Source of our being, can we come to that destiny for which we are created. Then, as Marcus Aurelius said, we shall "no longer talk about the kind of man that a good man ought to be — but be such!"

There is nothing supernatural about the control of destiny by the law of Mind. When it is thoroughly understood, it will be seen as spontaneously natural. Since Mind, Spirit, Causation, is Infinite, we can never encompass It — we can never grasp all of It — yet, we shall always be in God and of God. And Mind is One. There are not two minds, though we use two names in describing the classifications of Mind — the objective, or conscious; and the subjective, or unconscious. The subjective state of mind is that part of mind which is set in motion, as a creative thing, by the conscious mind. Or in other words, the subjective mind is the mental Law of our being, the creative force within our being. There are not two subjective minds. What we speak of as our subjective mind is really the use we make of the Universal Subjective Mind.

Thus we see that, within, there is a creative field that we call subjective mind, but this must not be thought of as actually an individual mind; it is *individualized*; and back of the individual point is the great, limitless, Universal Subjective Mind, operating as Law. The very simplest way we can state this is that we have a conscious mind which operates in a subjective field which is creative; the conscious mind is Spirit and the subjective mind is Law . . . one complementing the other, and the combination of both being expressed in every individuality. "No matter what our objective situation may be, there is always something inside of us which makes us realize that there is a Power within, which has never been violated, and which can lift us out of any unpleasant manifestation. This is the God within. Thus we see that in Spirit, conscious mind, we are one with God, and on the subjective we are one with Law." This must be so, since God is One, and being one with the Whole, we must be one with the Law of the Whole as well as the Spirit of the Whole.

This is nothing more than saying that good is universal and that as much good as any individual is able to incorporate in his life, is his to use. Then we might say that the mind, spirit and intelligence, which we find in ourselves this moment, is as much of the creative God as we understand. If God is to interpret Himself to man, He must interpret Himself through man . . . even Spirit is unable to make a gift which we will not accept. Do you begin to see now why we so evidently control our destiny? If we say we can only experience a little good, then — so complete is our freedom in this domain of thought, the power which appears to bind us being the only power in the universe which can free us — we shall experience but little good. Our *belief* sets the limit to the operation of a Principle which, in Its very nature, is without limit.

170

As much good *as we can believe* will come into our lives. How much good can we believe? We are thinking, willing, knowing, conscious centers of Life. We are surrounded by, immersed in, and there is flowing through us, a creative Something, which operates according to Law. And the dominating tendency of our thought — our strongest conviction — is what sets that in motion. *If we can believe that great good is ours now, we are setting in motion the very law which starts that good on its way to us.*

While it is true that we are dealing with Infinite Mind that knows all things; that is omniscient, omnipotent, and omnipresent; it is also true that this Intelligence cannot impart Its ideas to us unless we are willing to receive them. We must provide, through our receptive mentalities, an outlet through which Divine Mind can reveal to us Its knowledge and wisdom. What we draw from Mind — in which exists the potential of all knowledge — we must draw through the channels of our own minds. A conscious connection must be established. That is what is meant by "We can only know God as we become God." That means, naturally, as we partake of the Divine Nature, by believing in It and becoming receptive to It. The mechanical laws of nature are set and immutable, but the spontaneous recognition of these laws gives us the power to bring them into practical, everyday use. Love is the Divine Givingness; Law is the Way. That is why we say all is Love yet all is Law. An Infinite Spirit, operating through an impersonal, Infinite and Immutable Law. If the kingdom of God is within us, we should realize it now, for "Where the Spirit of truth is, there is liberty."

Undoubtedly, we are surrounded by and immersed in a perfect Life, a complete, normal, harmonious and peaceful existence. But only as much of this Life as we embody will really become ours to use. This is a tremendous and beautiful concept and proves, conclusively, that we do control our own destiny, making it important or insignificant, as we choose. Should we wish to know a certain truth, which we think is necessary to our next forward step, we should state that the truth is already known in Mind, which statement will be true. AS WE ACCEPT THIS, our mind will perceive the truth about that which we desire to know. This is how we are able to tap the Infinite Reservoir of Wisdom for any information which we need in our daily lives.

Someone may ask, can we bring forth both good and evil from the same Source? Of course not. The first premise on which we take our stand is that God is All and that God is Good; therefore, all is Good. So, only as our thought and action tends toward a constructive program will it eventually succeed. The Principle, as stated in Religious Science, is:

"We are surrounded by an Infinite possibility. It is Goodness, Life, Law and Reason. In expressing Itself through us, It becomes more fully conscious of Its own being. Therefore, It wishes to express through us. As It passes into our being, It automatically becomes the law of our lives. It can pass into expression through us only as we allow It to do so. Therefore, we should have faith in It and Its desires and ability to do all for us that we shall ever need to have done. Since It must pass through our consciousness to operate for us, we must be conscious that It is doing so."

We should be able to look at any wrong condition — any state or condition of affairs that we think is hindering our progress—with the knowledge that we can change it. This calls for a positive understanding of the Truth, a willing-ness to let this inner Spirit guide us. "The law of the Lord is perfect." (Ps. 19:7), and in so far as our belief is in line with this perfect law, nothing can hinder its accomplishment. As Jesus said: "Heaven and earth shall pass away, but my words shall not pass away." (Matt. 24:35)

Now, I would not have you become confused in this matter of controlling our destiny. It is not done by a passive wishing that so and so might happen. Merely wishing, hoping, always carries the thought that a thing might happen and it might not . . . but we hope it does. On the other hand, we must be very careful not to imagine that we create the *power* that brings things to pass. Our thought is creative only be-cause it makes the molds, the forms, into which our good is to be poured. It has nothing to do with creating the substance itself. That already exists as a part of the Universal Energy. But, if we wish a certain good, we must get in our minds a realization of this good, thereby placing in Mind the mold, which will be filled by the sub-stance necessary for the complete manifestation of this good in our lives. The Principle is perfect,

174

and when we compel our mind to perceive this perfection, it will automatically create for us.

How far can we depend on this? Will it produce for us, in the objective world, houses, bonds, lands, gold, friends, position, prestige? Is it possible for us to have any or all of these? Absolutely all of them, IF WE CAN EMBODY THEM! "It is done unto you as you believe." Over and over again, Jesus repeated this. The field through which thought operates is Infinite, but *we only know as much of this as we can prove!* That which we cannot prove may or may not be true, but there is no certainty in our minds about it until we can prove it. If we are deciding as our objective that we will be a person of great material wealth, that is all right. If we expect to eventually be a millionaire, there is no harm in that of itself. God does not know whether we are building one tiny little 12"window to allow the sunshine to come in, or whether we are building a modern home with windows all the way around. The sunshine is here and we can have all we wish. All of the water in the ocean belongs to one fish. God does not know whether we are now limiting our material wealth to one thousand or to one hundred thousand dollars a month. God's spiritual abundance is a fact, and the material wealth is only a symbol. We can have as much of the wealth as we can embody. If you have thought you could have only $200.00 a month, begin at once to think of twice or three times that amount. Set this law for yourself. As soon as you can get a complete embodiment of it, a complete sense of your having $500.00 or $600.00 a month, you will certainly bring this into your experience. As you realize this, it will increase your faith (increase your "substance of things not seen") and you will soon be able to visualize and embody a larger amount. By continual affirmation of your good as an ever-present reality, you will build up a belief strong enough to deliver to you any good you are able to think about. Enthrone in consciousness a desire worthy of your divinity, then in the peace of your soul sit back and *let* God do the work, thereby proving to the world, in incontrovertible results, that man controls his own destiny.

CHAPTER X

"Arise and Walk"

LESS THAN a hundred years ago, religion, to the average person, was something which required neither thought nor investigation. It was to be accepted because one's parents believed it right, without one's having any idea of what it was about . . . at least, no well-formed idea. But now with the increased mental activity throughout the world, people are no longer content to accept any teaching merely because someone says it is true. More and more, proof is being demanded for every statement that is made. At last, the world is beginning to think that people who call themselves Christians should so act that it will be easy to identify them . . . there should be "signs following," as Jesus said.

When Jesus sent his disciples out to declare the kingdom of God and to heal the sick, he didn't deceive them about what they were under-taking. He didn't tell them that the world would welcome them, for he knew that people who were revelling in the joys of sin would cling to their beliefs. He told them the truth they were about to declare would not bring peace, but a sword, to sinful beliefs, but in the face of this he gave them plenty of assurance: "I give unto you power to tread on serpents and scorpions, and over all the power of the enemy, and nothing by any means shall hurt you."

All metaphysicians recognize the fact that the healing of bodily ills is not the *most important* work of man, yet we believe it is the duty and privilege of man to follow the example of the Master. For us to call ourselves his followers and be content with a theoretical knowledge of the Christ-teaching, thereby living an inefficient life, is especially incongruous. We know, as Jesus knew, that disease is primarily the result of wrong thinking, and our *most important* work, with every person, should be to induce him to perceive his divine nature and think correctly.

This was shown when Jesus cured the man with palsy. He said: "But, that ye may know that the Son of man hath authority on earth to forgive sins (wipe out the effect of wrong thinking) . . . arise, take up thy bed and go into thy house."

178

It has been said, and truly, that a man's ability to cope with the problems of life is measured by his understanding of God. The deplorable mistakes in human history, which we classify as sickness, failure and disaster, will diminish in frequency and virulence, as we gain a better understanding of God as Mind, omnipresent, omnipotent and omniscient. The divine seed at the center of man contains the infinite possibilities of God. God not only created the idea (man) but He sustains it . . . but we are given choice in the matter. There is all around us everything that is necessary for complete fruition, but through wrong thinking, we can bring ourselves into decay if we wish.

The story goes that in Jerusalem, near the sheep gate, was the Pool of Bethesda, in which many cripples bathed, believing the waters of this pool had healing properties. The supposition was that an angel stirred the pool and he who *first* entered the water afterwards received healing; and there were porches built entirely around the pool where the halt, the lame, and the blind could lie, and wait for the time of entering the pool. A poor beggar had lain there 38 years! Jesus passed by and asked him if he wished to

179

be healed. "Always," he told Jesus, having no one to carry him to the water, "someone else reached the pool first." Had that been said to us, it is not unlikely we would have said, "I will see that someone carries you next time." But it was never Jesus' way to promise a man that he might be healed next week, or tomorrow, or next year. His was an immediate recognition of the omnipresence of God, an immediate perception that God was forever giving of Himself to man, as man would receive. When the beggar expressed his longing to be healed, Jesus' dynamic reply was "Arise, take up thy bed and walk."

The command is just as imperative to us today to cleanse our consciousness from everything that is unlike God. Many of us are astounded at that beggar. Wait 38 years for someone to carry us in? How ridiculous! Yet, many of us are doing just that. We are waiting for another to heal us, when all the while the Power is right within. But, before we can use this Power, we must know something about it. The man who knows nothing of the laws of electricity may do himself harm. If we are to heal ourselves, we must know *who* we are, and how the Power is used. The work of cleansing human consciousness is scientific and exact, not fortuitous and haphazard. The truth about God proves that He is perpetually reliable, never producing or allowing evil in any form. The truth concerning God's universe is that it partakes of His character.

"Sons of God, joint heirs with Jesus Christ," so the Bible reads, but to the consciousness who knows nothing of God, it doesn't carry special import. There are many of us who have been studying Truth for sometime, who still think of God as a super-man, resident in some far off place, who, if we pray to Him long enough, may heal us.

Before we can have any conception of the Power by which Jesus was able to see the perfect man in that beggar and say to him, "Arise, take up thy bed and walk," we shall have to understand that God is the very life *within us*. Not a Being afar off. The beggar had, to himself, all those 38 years, been giving the command, "Wait, wait until someone can carry you to the pool. Wait until someone can heal you." Jesus said, "Arise . . . and walk." We must come to the point where we know to a certainty that God is not love by itself, nor power by itself, nor life by itself, nor intelligence by itself, but God is the union of all of these, as someone has said "God is the union of all the potencies of life," *a union of all the powers to be*, and that God is right within. Often you hear God spoken of as "the great healing light." Can you now think of all these potencies within you, all of these essences of life, flowing and mingling together as a great flooding LIGHT?

It is a great joy to discover, in the study of divine law, that it is never partial, never evil, never unjust. The sick are healed and the sinful are reclaimed by the scientific understanding that there never has been, and never will be, a real law that can result in discord, disaster, accident, lack of disease. In our system of thought, we teach that God governs both man and the universe by means of orderly laws. Right thinking is law. This is a mighty force, and as servants of God, we must express it in our lives as practical and available in every emergency. Systematic, intelligent, and persistent mental work frees us from the argument of personal sense and opens wide the door to Infinite Wisdom. This is nothing more than the utilization of one's understanding of infinite intelligence in every circumstance of daily activity.

We have seen practically every ill of the body and every insanity of the mind healed by this understanding of the Omnipresence. We have seen it free people from cancer, tuberculosis, arthritis, blood poisoning, Bright's disease, blindness, deafness, nervous prostration, gall stones and a host of other ailments. We never refuse to treat a case because it has been pronounced "incurable." We know God's hand is not shortened, and He knows no more about a headache than he does a cancer. I recall when years ago I asked a teacher about our attitude toward malignant disease, and in reply she drew two ciphers for me, one large and one very small; and asked me which was the greater. I answered at once: "Why they have the same value, only one is small and the other large." "How do we regard all disease?" she asked. "As nothing," I said. Then she proceeded to explain how the small cipher might stand for a minor pain and the larger one might stand for a malignant disease, like cancer, but their value or lack of value would remain just the same. So, she said, the only thing for us to determine was how we would look at disease — as a reality or as an unreality; as a part of God's indestructible creation, or as a concept of man's false thinking. With the knowledge we now have, isn't it easy to see that no disease, curable or incurable, is a part of the kingdom of God?

Let us not wait until we think we have more power before we attempt to heal. If we do this, we shall never speak the healing word. The only thing necessary for perfect results is spiritual understanding, and the only time for its action is now. Treatment is solely a spiritual realization by which we see, in ourselves and others, the perfect Christ. No limitation of time, place or means, bounds the perfect demonstration of spirituality. We can talk about Truth and write about it, but we must realize its quickening, creative energy — the Truth which is the law of obliteration to anything unlike itself. Man being the offspring of the one Mind, must have the capacity in him to know that Mind . . . to know himself as the Infinite Mind, expressed. Then we shall be able to say "Arise . . . and walk," for we have the assurance carried in the Biblical promise: "There is a spirit in man, and the breath of the *Almighty* giveth them understanding."

CHAPTER XI

Is Fear Necessary?

THE MAN who stated to the world that fear is "perhaps the most conservative and constructive force in life" must have been referring to what is termed purely physiological fear, or what we call self-preservation — like the man who steps back in the street to avoid the passing motor car. Arguing from this standpoint, we will agree that it might be correct to assume that but for the fear of cold, men would not have built warmer houses; and but for the fear of famine, men would not have engaged in the back-breaking work of tilling the soil. In *that* sense, fear, might be termed "necessary to the advancement of civilization." This, however, is not the general acceptance of the word "fear": such aspects of civilization's progress might better be called that necessity, which became "the mother of invention."

Fear usually conveys to the mind that senseless, paralyzing, disorganizing emotion, which

185

undermines the moral fiber, weakens endurance, saps vitality, kills initiative and, in general, is the forerunner of disaster. It is the great skeleton in the closet, which every man tries to keep behind locked doors, but which is forever running ahead of him to trip him. Dr. Abraham Myerson, Professor of Neurology at Tufts College, says that every physician and every man in charge of the morale of soldiers is aware that *"what he has to combat is not only the fear of death and injury but the illnesses which arise from that fear, and the illnesses which come from the fear of showing fear."**

In recent years, internationally-known physicians have publicly admitted that fear, anger and worry bring disastrous effects upon the body mechanism, and explain many bodily impairments and diseases, but each century goes on having its outstanding fear, its plagues, and thousands of remedies are proposed by men, who divide fears into classes and give them names. We claim the greatest deliverance man stands in need of today is the deliverance from fear, and nothing but a knowledge of God, as ever-available Good, can offer a final remedy.

*Why Men Fail, p. 279.

The elimination of fear from the human consciousness is an important feature in the work of Religious Science, and we have repeatedly proven that as man is given an inspiration that lifts him out of his fear, he has taken a long step toward recovery. Also, it is frequently observed that people who are habitually free from fear and worry are less susceptible to illness than others. If we are to carry the banner of Truth, we must keep our minds free from the fears of the multitude.

When it has been discovered that fear is the mental cause of diseased bodily conditions manifested physically, of what avail is the knife upon the physical, with the mental cause still remaining? And what remedy does Religious Science employ for the emotion of fear? What does Infinite Mind do? It cannot possibly create a remedy which is not spiritual. The one remedy, in every case, is the understanding that Truth destroys every false belief; and as we explained, fear *is* a false belief because it is faith in a power which does not exist, a power opposed to Good. Fear is not, as we have believed, the opposite of faith; it is the other end of the same stick; it is faith misplaced.

187

Men claim they have tried to overcome their fear by will-power and determination, but have failed miserably. Small wonder. Someone remarked that trying to get rid of fear by will-power alone is "like trying to keep the ocean back with a shovel or trying to chase clouds away with a broom." There is no way you can frighten fear. The only thing you can do is to change its course. Remember fear is faith turned in the wrong direction. The only thing to do is to focus this emotion on the One and only Power, Good, and its current will be purified. For centuries, St. John has been telling us that "Perfect Love casteth out fear." That is the only remedy, on earth or in heaven, whereby man can be saved from fear. In that perfect love, fear-tormented men find a panacea that is "as free as the air, as animating as the sunrise, and as dependable as the tide of the sea." Fear may produce illness, but love is always healing; love is always creative; love is always uplifting.

We might write thousands of words, only to reiterate the statement, that the more of God we bring into consciousness, the less of fear can enter. Then, fill your heart with gladness and rule in your own domain, as "joint heir with Jesus Christ."

CHAPTER XII

The Power of the Presence

THERE IS something in the heart of man which can never be satisfied with any less than the full realization of his oneness with God. All that Jesus taught was for the purpose of directing men to the consciousness of their oneness with the Father . . . that they might find the kingdom of heaven within themselves. The *understanding* for which Solomon prayed was the revelation of God within the soul.

Jehovah told Moses to say "I AM THAT I AM . . . hath sent me unto you." We can say it with the same meaning today. Jesus' prayer for unity, "that they may all be one, even as thou, Father *art* in me, and I in thee, that they also may be in us . . . that they may be one even as we *are* one; I in them, and thou in me, that they may be perfected into one." One Life, One Intelligence, One Mind, One Truth, One Presence, One Power! "The kingdom of God is nigh," and God is One. That One is now and forever the same, the Spirit of what is true, of what is alive with goodness, with love, with perfection, and with the purpose to express these ends.

Every word written in this book, up to this point, has been for the sole purpose of imparting to you the assurance that there is a Power within, *which is the answer to all our problems.* Whether we call it the Power of the Presence or the presence of the Power, we are referring to the I AM consciousness — the Christ consciousness, which Jesus so perfectly embodied and which we are daily striving to more completely realize. This embodiment of the spirit of Christ must include that understanding which recognizes that "all things whatsoever the Father hath are mine."

If we become conscious of the fact that no matter what we are doing — plowing or pruning, mining or marketing, acquiring knowledge or imparting information — it is God working through us, it will revolutionize our lives. When we are conscious of His Presence; and we know that He is the source of all good, then nothing can prevent Him from manifesting through us as *any* good that we can imagine.

If God is Omnipresence, then He is present in every cell in our body, and *as we recognize this,*

He will manifest as perfection in every part of us. "If we could stand aside and let the One Perfect Life flow through us, we could not help healing others."

The only One-ness there is is the consciousness of the omnipresence of Good. All of us are one with each other because we are that One Consciousness of God, which is the only one-ness there can ever be. When we say *consciousness*, we mean reality, not belief. What seems to make all discord and lack is the conflict between idea and belief. Man is wholly good and beliefs are no part of consciousness, but only a claim of the absence of consciousness, but right where the belief seems to be, IDEA is — Omnipresence is.

The Lamp we have been attempting to lift for you is the Presence of God, the Presence of Power, the Presence of Authority, the Presence of Wisdom, the Presence of Joy. Paul refers to the "Christ in you, the hope of glory." As someone has said, "Christ is God's idea of man . . . God's anointed, or God's thought of a perfect man, implanted in the spiritual being of every man. We can better comprehend this, as we remember that God is the One Creative Mind, the Source of all existence. Man is the result of the greatest grouping of ideas — or the greatest idea — in Divine Mind." As we appropriate the God-implanted ideas, such as love, life, wisdom, justice, tenderness, patience, power, and understanding, we develop a better use of our Godlike power, which is I AM.

If you can but grasp the simplicity of the fact of the Presence of God working in you . . . operating in and through *all* your affairs . . . you will only need to direct your desire to what you would see manifest. The generating power of this dynamo is Love. The acknowledgment of this divine power, this I AM Presence, is sufficient to bring into expression anything you wish. "I AM wealth." "I AM health." "I AM power." As you say "I AM" you are acknowledging the Power against which there is no resistance. When I say "I AM" I have set in motion the only Power there is which can accomplish that whereunto it is sent. "The Father that dwelleth in me, he doeth the works," was the manner in which Jesus identified his work with the Father; so, as we recognize Christ as "the author and finisher of our faith," we are enabled to look away from personal efforts and claim grace and ability according to the gift of Christ.

In *Science of Mind,* we read:

"In moments of deepest realization, the great mystics have sensed that one Life flows through ALL; that all are some part of that life. They have also seen Substance, a fine, white, brilliant stuff, forever falling into everything; a Substance indestructible and eternal. At times, the realization has been so complete that they have been actually blinded by the LIGHT. There are instances, where for several days after the experience, the one having it could not see on the physical plane; for he had seen the INNER LIGHT . . . In flashes of illumination, the inspired have seen INTO THE VERY CENTER OF REALITY, and have brought back with them a picture of what they have seen and felt. This has not been illusion, for ALL HAVE SEEN THE SAME THING."

One with the whole, One with each other, and at the same time God personified, God individualized. "To understand the life of Jesus the Christ from the high plane of unity with God, is to see all life as God sees and knows it — perfect, abundant, pure, holy, free."

We will know and understand Jesus the Christ only through the divine qualities we have unfolded: "Let this mind be in you, which was also in Christ Jesus; who being in the form of God,

193

thought it not robbery to be equal with God."
(Phil. 2:5, 6.) As we understand this union with
Christ—the I AM Presence within us—our own
word and works become powerful. Jesus proved
his Oneness with God. "Living in daily recognition of our own divinity, and the divinity of
the whole, we will rise above criticism, condemna-
tion, and fault-finding, and even above talking
too much on spiritual subjects. We will grow
thoughtful, and creative. The true life does not
consist in the ability to talk the truth, but in
living it."

Someone has said, "We are here for one purpose — to manifest God, the Good. Therefore,
we will not consider energy, time, devotion or
love wasted, which has been, or will be, used to
bring about the finished result. Every aspiration,
word, thought, or act, which has been given to
this ideal, was necessary to its fulfillment." If
divinity is One, then where He is in consciousness, we may be. Truth is not a patch to be used
to mend some old worn-out religious creed. It is
the whole seamless garment and will perfectly
clothe and fit the one who fearlessly claims his
divinity.

While all I have written has been to *lead* you

194

to the consciousness of this Presence, it is not within my power to *reveal* it to you. Every man must find it for himself, within his own soul. Emerson, in speaking of the God within us, said:

"This energy (generated by the consciousness of God in the soul)* does not descend into individual life on any other condition than entire possession. It comes to the lowly and simple; it comes to whoever will put off what is foreign and proud; it comes as insight; it comes as serenity and grandeur. When we see those whom it inhabits, we are apprised of new degrees of greatness. From that inspiration (consciousness of Oneness with God) the man comes back with a changed tone. He does not talk with men with an eye to their opinion; he . . . is plain and true; has no rose color, no friends . . . no advantages; does not want admiration; dwells in the hour that now is."

I would call your attention to the expression *entire possession.* We may be looking only for health, and get it, but only *as we desire the complete essence of Good* will we be able to pass this good on to others, or grasp the full significance of *entire possession* . . . the full significance of the wholeness of the I AM.

---

*(Parenthetical explanations not part of original quotation.)

195

We lift our lamp that you may be willing to take the first step; that you may be led to say to yourself, "I will arise and go unto my Father," and then you will shortly know that He forever desires to manifest Himself within you, as your present deliverance from all disturbing conditions; you will press on past the place of doubt. "You will not longer dwell in darkness, for the LIGHT will be within your own soul; you will be conscious of a new and diviner life in your body and a new and diviner love for all people, a new and diviner power to accomplish."

We must so feel our oneness with the Christ consciousness — the great I AM — that we can realize at any minute that God is our perfect supply — of health, power, intelligence or joy — and ready to manifest in our lives any moment we decree. As Mrs. Cady says: "We want such a revelation of God as love, within us . . . a love that will flow with the spontaneity and fullness of an artesian well, because it is so full at the bottom that it *must* flow out." Then comes to the soul of man the inner revelation of "*my* Lord and *my* God." The Christ then dwells within us and we see that the LIGHT we have been praying for is not a thing; it is God Himself. Thus we come to the conscious, active taking of what God is always giving — the divine substance flowing in at the center and out into the visible — and we arrive at the necessity for spontaneous praise of this inner Presence, this Presence which blesses us, as we *abide* in the Secret Place of the Most High. Can you not see that, no matter what the problem, the only task is to "wait thou upon God?" I do not need to give you suggestions for the ordering of your life. If you will practice casting your problems in the lap of the Indwelling Presence, the I AM, all solutions will be made according to the Christ Mind. You will *have* the Power of the Presence! As a final thought, I would leave with you a quotation from Ernest Holmes' article on Realization:

"There is a point in the supreme moment of realization, where the individual merges with the Universe, but not to the loss of his individuality; where a sense of Oneness of all life so enters his being, that there is no sense of otherness; it is here that the mentality performs seeming miracles, because there is nothing to hinder the whole from coming through."

Are you attracted to this "Secret place of the Most High?" This is the place where we meet

Christ, at the center of our being; and this place must be found by each one for himself. If you would have this Power of the Presence, prove whether the prophecy of Isaiah is true: "And if thou draw out thy soul to the hungry, and satisfy the afflicted soul; then shall thy LIGHT rise in obscurity, and thy darkness be as noonday."